Faith in Dialogue

Faith in Dialogue

A Christian
Apologetic

Jerry H. Gill

JARRELL

A SPECIAL IMPRINT
OF
WORD BOOKS

FAITH IN DIALOGUE: A CHRISTIAN APOLOGETIC

Scripture quotations, unless otherwise specified, are from the King James Version. Those marked rsv are from The Revised Standard Version of the Bible, copyright © 1946, 1952, © 1971 and 1973 by the Division of Christian Education of the National Council of the Churches of Christ in the U.S.A., and are used by permission.

Library of Congress Cataloging-in-Publication Data:

    Gill, Jerry H.
      Faith in dialogue.

      Bibliography: p.
      1. Apologetics—20th century. I. Title.
    BT1102.G53   1985   239   85-17818
    ISBN 0-8499-0495-1

Printed in the United States of America

5 6 7 8 9 8   RRD   9 8 7 6 5 4 3 2 1

For the Sorri family, with love

Contents

Faith in Dialogue

Setting the Stage: 1
A Matter of Posture

IN THE TRADITIONAL SENSE of the term "apologetic," this is not one. When developing an apologetic for the Christian faith, people generally have sought to set forth a rationale for belief and commitment, offering reasons why one ought to be a Christian and meeting objections raised by those who are opposed to religious belief. Unfortunately, those engaged in such projects often take either an aggressive or a defensive posture, ignoring conflicting evidence and/or adopting a dogmatic tone. Somehow this approach has always struck me as being out of harmony with the nature of Christian faith itself.

In addition, the unspoken assumption behind many traditional apologetics is that Christian faith is essentially parallel to scientific belief in that both are matters of drawing valid conclusions from available data. Thus, the only issue is a quantitative one, namely whether or not there is sufficient evidence to warrant belief. Aside from the fact that this assumption grossly distorts the nature of scientific reasoning, traditional apologetics usually fails to take up questions pertaining to the nature of the reasoning process itself, the complexity of the crucial concepts involved, and the possibility of an open-ended faith such as that expressed by the man who said to Jesus, "I believe; help my unbelief" (Mark 9:24, RSV).

On the other hand, there are those who disdain the apologetic task altogether, either because they believe that Christian faith is entirely a gift of God or because they advocate religious commitment as a "leap of faith." Such thinkers would quote Pascal: "The heart has reasons that reason knows not of." What those who take this approach overlook is that it proves too much. If Christian belief is justified by faith alone, then so is every other form of belief on the commitment market, since the devotees of each are equally convinced they are right. Besides, it is important to notice that Pascal still called the reasons which are not known by reason, "reasons." He was not contrasting faith to reason, but by means of this play on words was making a proposal for understanding reason itself in a broader and deeper fashion.

Against the backdrop of these standard postures toward apologetics, I should like to invite the reader to take up a more *dialogical* posture when reasoning about Christian faith, whether approaching it as a believer or as an unbeliever. It is my conviction that the only apologetic appropriate both to the nature of Christian belief and to the pluralistic character of our times is one which is open enough to acknowledge the limitations of religious knowledge and faith as well as to affirm their reasonableness. We must remember that even believers "see through a glass, darkly," and that there is no inherent contradiction between confidence and humility.

As I understand it, a dialogical posture is one that takes the matters of religious reality and truth so seriously as to require extreme openness to and growth *toward* them, as well as radical sincerity and commitment *to* them. Thus, all sides and aspects of an issue must be explored with humble thoroughness, and whatever is deemed worthy of commitment must be incorporated into one's life with integrity.

Moreover, a dialogical posture is one that *listens* as well as shares. Faith in God is open to truth wherever it is encountered; it takes both the questions raised and the answers given by unbelievers extremely seriously. To put all this another way, authentic Christian faith, as I understand it, has nothing to fear from interchange with those of differing points of view. One must have confidence that God's truth

will vindicate itself to those who seek it sincerely; it does not
need to be defended. A faith based in fear is like a faith
without works; it is not faith at all.

One of the most tragic patterns to be observed within the
Christian community is the one wherein people, especially
young people, are given to believe that in matters religious
one has nothing unless one has absolute certainty. Then,
when genuine difficulties and puzzles arise—and they inevitably do—the only conclusion to draw is that one's faith must
be inauthentic or that it must be set aside. In twenty-five
years of teaching I have witnessed the negative yet unnecessary results of this false dilemma time and time again. The
aim of this book is to avoid this "all or nothing" way of
thinking by acknowledging at the outset that faith will always
be confronted with unresolved mysteries, by defining faith
not as "believing what you know isn't true," but as a life of
trust and faithfulness in the face of many difficulties and am-
biguities.

In a sense, *Faith in Dialogue* is offered in response to the
position taken by the early Christian leader Tertullian when
he asked, "What has Athens to do with Jerusalem?" Tertullian meant the question rhetorically, with the implied answer
a flat "Nothing!" His position was a separatist one in the
sense that he saw no connection, especially in matters of the
truth about reality and human destiny, between the wisdom
of humanity and the revelation of God in the Judeo-Christian
faith. (Athens was taken to symbolize the highest strivings of
human reason, while Jerusalem was viewed as the symbol of
revealed truth.) Tertullian and others like him saw no need
for further reasoning about such matters, since God had
clearly spoken the final word.

The theme of the present explorations, however, is that
rational Athens and faithful Jerusalem have much in common
and much to say to each other. The posture is thus one of
Athens *and* Jerusalem, of dialogical interaction between our
God-given capacity to think and the revelatory activity of
God in nature, history, and community. The approach taken

here is clearly within the tradition of "natural theology" in the sense that it assumes that reason, when more broadly and deeply defined, plays an important role in our knowledge of the divine, whether generally or specifically conceived.

Some special clarification is in order here. In contrast to Tertullian's "faith alone" posture, there are three other classical postures developed by great thinkers of the church. At the opposite extreme is the position of "reason alone," taken by those who deny the possibility of special divine activity within human experience. Some Arabian Moslem thinkers took this approach in the Middle Ages, as did the philosophers Locke, Kant, and Hegel, famous as proponents of the "Age of Reason." In my judgment, this posture is, on the one hand, far too confident of the ability of human rationality to comprehend mystery, and on the other, much too limited in its understanding of rationality. We shall return to this theme later on.

Between these two extremes stand those who either affirm the priority of faith *over* reason while acknowledging the necessity of the latter when based *in* faith, or who affirm the primacy of reason when complemented by faith. Anselm and Augustine took the former position, summarized in the motto, "We must believe *in order* to understand." Aquinas took the latter position when he developed a "separate but equal" approach to the relation between reason and faith. He maintained that some things, namely divine existence and power, can be known about God by means of unaided reason, while others, such as the nature and reality of God's redemptive love, can be known only through revelation.

The difficulties with the former view center around the possible definitions of the "belief" that must precede understanding. For if it is taken to mean giving assent within a cognitive vacuum, then it falls victim to the same criticisms as does Tertullian's view. If, on the other hand, it is defined as a broadened concept of reason, following Pascal's suggestion, then the way is opened for a more thorough and helpful approach to the relation between reason and faith. Thus the appropriateness of the theme, "Athens *and* Jerusalem." I shall try to develop such an understanding in chapter 7.

The difficulties with the latter view, that of Aquinas, center around the narrowness of the conception of reason as essentially a deductive enterprise by means of which one *proves* God's existence (hence the "classical proofs" for God's existence, including Aquinas's "Five Ways"). Also, there is the difficulty of establishing that a revelation of divine reality is present in the Judeo-Christian religion, since belief in the reliability of miracles, the Bible, and the church is subject to a great deal of debate. Here again, a great deal of progress can be made if reason is defined more broadly and flexibly, while faith is seen more as a total way of life (including, to be sure, a way of thinking) rather than as simple mental assent to a given set of propositions. More about this in chapter 7 as well.

The upshot of all of this is that I am suggesting that a dialogical approach, one that focuses on a functional, interactive relationship between reason and faith (Athens *and* Jerusalem), is more helpful than the more traditional postures. After all, God gave us minds and reasoning capacities, and even a view which contends that the image of God in us has been destroyed or hopelessly perverted must use reason to *understand* and *expound* this view itself. Even Paul, when arguing that the foolishness of God (and of the Christian faith) is wiser than human wisdom (1 Cor. 3:13), used rational language and argument to make his case. Furthermore, he, like Pascal, still called God's wisdom "wisdom," and it is only through our mental processes that we can understand *what* he means and *follow* his argument.

There is one further consideration that renders the dialogical posture more fruitful than the more common ones. It should be remembered that all of the standard approaches to the relation between faith and reason were developed within what we call "the Christian era." That is to say, each one of these approaches was worked out in a time and place in which Western culture and Christianity were largely synonymous. The basic issue was belief versus unbelief *within* Christendom. (The two minor exceptions to this are Tertullian's posture, which was developed before Christianity became the "official" religion of the Roman Empire—thus its basic defensive character—and Aquinas's view, which arose in confrontation with Islam.) Today our situation is entirely different. Not only are there many essentially distinct paths of faith and nonfaith calling for our commitment, but the need for tolerance and mutual understanding has never been greater. In fact, it would seem that a dialogical posture is essential to our very survival, both as a culture and as a species.

All of this is extremely well focused in colleges and universities, where the search for knowledge of reality is growing ever more complex and urgent. To be sure, much of this search is confused and arrogant, but this in no way justifies "ostrich-headedness" on the part of Christians. Rather, the continual and exciting challenge facing the Christian student today is to work out a meaningful and fruitful relationship between his or her faith and all these issues and perspectives—one which is neither defensive nor uncritical. The purpose of this book is to assist in this task. It is written from *within* the academic community, believing in the intrinsic value of the academic enterprise despite its limitations. It is written on *behalf* of Christian students who are committed to working out a viable and vital relationship between their reason and their faith, between Athens *and* Jerusalem, without fudging on either.

The shape of this particular dialogical exploration is structured around the main areas or divisions of academic endeavor, such as natural science, social science, and the humanities. Chapters 2 through 6 will examine some of the pressing issues within each of these fields, with an eye to discerning how they bear upon Christian belief and vice versa. Dialogue, rather than attack or defense, will be the goal, for the assumption is that each community has much to learn from the other. It must be remembered, of course, that this is only an *initial* exploration, and that in two separate senses. First, it is initial in the sense that space will only permit an introduction to the crucial issues. Moreover, the aim is to *model* the dialogical posture, not to provide final answers for others to accept. Second, this is an initial exploration in the sense that for all of us the dialogue between reason and faith is, necessarily, an ongoing one. This is true not only because our reason is limited and knowledge is forever increasing (or at least changing!), but because faith, too, is always growing, seeking to become more and more mature.

After engaging the main academic disciplines and the crucial issues pertaining to their relationship to Christian belief, I shall offer (chapter 7) a brief introduction to a fresh philosophical perspective which I take to provide the most fruitful axis around which to organize our understanding of the relation between faith and reason. The focus of this perspective is worked out in greater detail in an earlier book entitled *On Knowing God* (Westminster Press, 1981). Those who want to pursue these matters further may wish to examine that book. The hope is that by providing a different philosophical axis for the crucial issues under consideration, we shall be enabled to return to them (briefly, in chapter 8) with increased insight and integrity—that faith and reason, when properly conceived, will be understood not as enemies or as distant cousins but as colaborers in the search for and response to God's truth. As Paul puts it in his letter to the Colossians (1:18), Christ should have the preeminence *"in* all things," not above or over against all things. Clearly this includes our minds as well as our hearts.

Although my own work in philosophy and religion has continuously led me into dialogue with a wide variety of other fields and issues, there is no sense in which I am an expert with respect to all of them. I am committed to an interdisciplinary exploration of truth, and I shall do my very best to present the issues as accurately and as fairly as possible. In the final analysis, however, my primary concern is to engage readers in dialogue so as to enable them to enter into the ongoing discussion on their own. The success of this task does not hinge on whether or not I have all my facts and moves right, but on the degree to which this exploration challenges the reader to participate in the dialogical process and contributes to the quality of that participation. I would submit that such participation is at some level essential to, if not synonymous with, that interactive process known as faith.

Before concluding this introductory chapter, let me say a word about two issues which *might* well be treated in a book such as this, but which will *not* be dealt with—the one because it is more precisely a philosophical concern than a religious one, the other because it is more a problem for theology *per se* than for a general discussion of the relation between faith and the academy. Both issues are of real interest and importance in their own right, and both have indirect bearing on our general theme. Nevertheless, it seems wisest to mention them here but not to take them up in the text itself.

The first issue I have in mind is that of the relation between artificial intelligence and the human mind. One of the most intriguing questions of our day is whether or not we should call what computers do "thinking." If we say no to this question, we must be able to say *why*, and this is not as easy as many think it is. If we say yes, then we are left wondering about the nature of human thought *and* about human nature in general. It is at this juncture that this issue comes into contact with religious belief. For traditionally, religious thinkers and believers have affirmed the existence of the human soul as something which is other and more than the physical body that "houses" it, and which accounts for human thought. If machines think, do they have souls? If not, do we?

Without going into any detail, let me ever so briefly indicate two moves that might prove helpful here for one who is interested in a Christian approach to this issue. To begin with, there has been a good deal of biblical and theological scholarship in recent years aimed at showing that the traditional soul-body dichotomy is far more a classic Greek idea than a Christian one (see especially J. A. T. Robinson's *The*

Body, SCM Press, 1977, and Robert Nelson's *Embodiment,* Augsburg Press, 1980). If we do not think of the human person as a soul *in* a body, or as having *parts* in the first place, perhaps a good deal of the confusion surrounding this issue would disappear. The Scriptures tend to use the terms "person," "soul," and "body" as synonymous (see Rom. 12:1–2, for example).

Also, there are serious difficulties with talking about computers thinking. There seems to be a qualitative difference between the kind of work they do and that of which humans are capable. The reason for this is that while a machine needs an explicitly formulated program to follow, the highest form of human intelligence functions without such a program. A case in point is the fact that although chess-playing computers generally beat good chess players, none has ever *come close* to beating a chess *master.* The latter frequently make decisions without checking out the various possibilities, while the computer operates by rote. There are even those who make a convincing case that computers cannot be said to think, not because they do not have *minds,* but because they do not have *bodies.* That is, they do not participate in nor interact with the world (see Herbert Dreyfus, *What Computers Can't Do,* University of California Press, 1979).

The second issue we shall not take up is the so-called "problem of evil." Even though it is extremely significant, (in fact it is frequently said to be the number-one stumbling block to Christian belief), technically speaking it is primarily a problem for theologians because it hinges on one's definition of God. The difficulty arises as soon as God is defined as both all-powerful and perfectly loving—which is the way Christians have traditionally defined God. If God is conceived of in this way, how are we to explain the presence of evil—especially suffering—in the world? It would seem either that God *could* do something about evil, but *will* not (in which case God can hardly be said to be perfectly loving), or that God *would* do something about evil, but *cannot* (in which case God is clearly not all-powerful).

There are many standard—and some not so standard—

ways of treating this problem, but this is not the place to go into them (a good book to consult is John Hick's *Evil and The God of Love*). In my opinion, the best possibility for a responsible treatment of this difficulty lies in the following approach: A perfectly loving God would want human beings to be loving as well. True love is based on *choice*, not coercion. So, people must be free in order to love. True freedom entails the possibility of choosing wrongly, and when we choose wrongly (against the Creator's loving will and our own best interests), we cause evil and suffering for ourselves as well as for other human beings.

It should be noted, of course, that even if this line of thought is helpful with respect to what is called "moral evil," it still leaves the question of "natural evil" (earthquakes, plagues, etc.) pretty much unexplained. I have some thoughts on this subject as well, but it is time to get started on what we came here to do. Using what I must admit to be a bad pun, "sufficient unto the day is the evil thereof," I invite the reader to join in the dialogue between Athens and Jerusalem.

Suggested Reading

Gill, J. *On Knowing God.* Philadelphia: Westminister, 1981.

Gilson, E. *Reason and Revelation in the Middle Ages.* New York: Scribner, 1938.

Johnson, R. et al. *Critical Issues in Modern Religion.* Englewood Cliffs, NJ: Prentice-Hall, 1973.

Niebuhr, H. R. *Christ and Culture.* New York: Harper & Row, 1951.

Natural Science: 2
Reductionism

THE HISTORY OF THE "OFFICIAL" CHRISTIAN STANCE toward the natural sciences has not been good. From the time of Galileo through that of Newton to that of Darwin, Christian leaders and thinkers have either pitted theology against current discoveries and theories or they have essentially equated the scientific status quo with theological truth. In either case subsequent developments have shown such postures to be embarrassing at best and downright pernicious at worst. Scientists, too, have frequently heralded their experiments and deductions as establishing the falsehood and demise of religious belief. Hopefully we all have learned from this history that the issues involved here are very complex and that a good deal of caution is called for.

In recent years it has become popular to avoid the conflicts between science and religion by defining them as having absolutely *nothing* to do with each other. The one is said to deal with tangible, factual, and objective reality, while the other is claimed to treat intangible, valuational, and subjective reality. In my own opinion, this neat dichotomy, promoted largely by existentialist thinkers, purchases cognitive peace at too great a price—namely a sort of schizophrenic existence in which one's faith has absolutely nothing to do with one of the more important and indispensable dimensions of human experience. Thus, while I would not advocate viewing science' and

21

religion as essentially doing the same thing, it seems every bit as disatrous to define them as entirely separate.

In this chapter I shall take up several of the more pressing issues that arise in the dialogue between natural science and Christian faith, seeking to shed light in both directions at once. Once again it should be noted that the limitations of both space and knowledge will keep the discussion at an abstract level. The central concern is not with specific data and answers, but rather with a particular way of coming at the issues, namely, the dialogical mode.

CREATION AND NATURAL SELECTION

The question of origins is one that has always interested scientists and religious thinkers alike. More specifically, the origin of the universe and the origin of the human species are important issues for both fields. The Judeo-Christian faith has traditionally maintained that God created the universe "in the beginning" and that humanity is the highest expression of this creation, having come into existence *sui generis* or in a manner quite distinct from that of the animal kingdom. The first two chapters of the Book of Genesis are the main source of these beliefs. They have been challenged both by philosophers ancient and modern (many of whom have maintained that the universe is eternal), and by scientists who argue that humankind evolved from less complex forms of life through the process of natural selection.

In recent years a great deal has been made of the so-called "big bang" theory developed by astrophysicists to account for the origin of the universe. On the basis of the fact that the universe is expanding at an extremely high velocity, it has been concluded that it must have begun as one huge mass of gas, matter, and energy which exploded into the galaxies and solar system as we know them. Religious thinkers have frequently used this theory as substantiation of the creationist account of the universe's origin, as a scientific way to describe the opening verses of Genesis. While there is no way to settle this question with any finality now (or ever, perhaps), there are several points that can and need to be made along the way.

To begin with, it is important to bear in mind that just because our universe is presently involved in an expanding process it by no means follows that it had a specific beginning. It is entirely possible that such expansion is simply one phase of a two-phase contraction/expansion cycle, and that this cycle has been repeating itself forever. Moreover, even if this particular pattern of the universe did begin with a "big bang" from an incredibly concentrated mass, it is still possible to ask "Where did this mass come from and what form was it in prior to that?" Most astrophysicists would point out that the question of origins, in this sense of the term, is not a scientific issue.

Coming at this question from another angle, it is helpful to ask whether the Genesis narrative is in fact meant to be taken as any kind of empirical account of how the universe began. If one were to come across this story, without having been told that it is part of sacred Scripture, it does not seem likely that it would be natural to interpret it as a scientific document. The language is very symbolic, with God speaking, dividing between day and night prior to creating the sun and the moon, walking in the garden, etc. Moreover, there are at least two separate accounts of the order of creation (Gen. 1 and 2), the one placing human origins last and the other placing them first. In addition, the verb that is used for the creative act is related to the Hebrew term denoting human acts of fashioning and shaping material already at hand, rather than implying any notion of creating "*ex nihilo*" (out of nothing).

It would seem that the intent of the opening chapters of Genesis (1–11), as distinguished from the remaining chapters, is to stress divine responsibility and concern for the universe and humankind, rather than to give a detailed, scientific account of their origin. To be sure, this does not mean that there cannot be a certain degree of harmony between patterns suggested in the Genesis story and those discoverable and/or hypothesized by scientists. It is only to suggest that the purposes of the two approches to the question of origins are neither identical nor necessarily in conflict.

It is also helpful to note, when moving on to the question of the origin of life on our planet, that the Hebrew word translated "day" in the various days of creation in Genesis is a general term signifying a given time span, including but not necessarily limited to a twenty-four hour period. The word is sometimes used to refer to unspecified time in the future ("the day of the Lord") and sometimes to a broad historical or psychological event (e.g., "Every dog has its day"). Thus, it is quite possible to harmonize the day-by-day account of creation given in Genesis with a scientific description of the probable stages of the development of life on earth.

In fact, there are those who suggest that the best way to coordinate these two approaches is by means of what may be called "threshold evolution." The idea here is that although there is good reason to believe that there has been a great deal of evolution by natural selection *within* the boundaries of the various phyla of life, there may not have been any evolution across the thresholds separating these phyla from one another. On the other hand, there are scientists who dispute this claim. It must be borne in mind, especially with respect to the origins of the human species, that scientists disagree among themselves a great deal. This is particularly true since the recent archaeological discoveries of the Leakey family and Donald Johanson.[1]

The disagreement among scientists does not indicate a weakness in the scientific enterprise, but rather reminds us that all human endeavors are approximate at best. This includes theology as well. If there are mistakes and frauds within the scientific community, they are revealed by further scientific activity, not by appealing to theological authority. Both fields must be careful not to overstep their bounds and make pronouncements which are inappropriate to their purposes. At the same time, however, those working in both fields should be in dialogue with one another, if only to help each other chart the vague and ever-shifting boundaries between them.

Much of the discussion about the relation between science and religion hinges on the distinction between induction and deduction. In the former, one begins with particular data and moves toward more or less probable general conclusions, while in the latter, one begins with general principles and moves to certain (or self-contradictory) particular conclusions. Scientists often forget that they are limited by their commitment to induction to making probability statements. Theologians often forget that it is possible, and perhaps advisable, to think of theology as an inductive process. Much depends here, of course, on whether one thinks of theology as revealed or as part of the human response to revelation. The latter view seems more nearly correct to me, and it is the foundation upon which my overall dialogical posture is based.

On the whole I see no difficulty with the position that maintains that God's creative powers and care have been expressed through the various stages of the evolutionary process. This does not in any way detract from God's greatness or goodness; in fact in some ways it magnifies them by filling in the concrete, intricate details of divine power, wisdom, and care throughout the entire creative enterprise. Without going so far as to divinize the evolutionary process, as perhaps Pierre Teilhard de Chardin has done, it is possible to affirm God's creative activity in and through this process without in any way compromising the fundamental intent of the creation story as found in Genesis. The former can be viewed as the *how* of creation while the latter can be acknowledged as the *why* of creation.

At the same time, however, there are two main difficulties that I see with the theory of evolution as an explanation of the development of the human species. The first has to do with the attempt to account for the highly specialized features of human life by means of natural selection alone. Some of the more complex and sophisticated functions exhibited by Homo sapiens seem unexplainable strictly in terms of any *necessity* of adaptation to the environment. Loren Eiseley,[2] a world-renowned scholar, has suggested that the size and intricacies of the human brain, for instance, far exceed what would be necessary for the survival and flourishing of the species. Also, our incredibly long period of dependency, the phenomenon of culture, and uniquely human face-to-face copulation all suggest the cruciality of the social dimension of human life, a dimension that would seem to transcend mere natural selection.

A second difficulty I have with evolutionary explanations of humankind is a bit more philosophical. There is an inherent *ad hoc* flavor to these explanations, whenever such anomolies as those mentioned above are raised for consideration. The tendency is simply to fall back on the assumption that all of the conditions constituting the context of our present universe have remained the same for eons and eons. Now, not only is such a move a bit question-begging (in that mere references to almost unending periods of time do not comprise an explanation of anything whatsoever), but it is entirely possible that our solar system may not always have been ordered as it is now, or at least may have been interrupted by other astrophysical bodies. These interruptions might well have altered such things as our protective shield against radiation from the sun (the so-called Van Allen belt), thereby making genetic alterations almost inevitable. These alterations, in turn, might well explain "missing links" between species, thereby making possible a form of "threshold evolution."

ATOMISM AND TELEOLOGY

Let us now refocus our attention on the study of the subatomic level of physical reality and its bearing on matters of religious belief. There was a time when physical science was perceived to be the primary enemy of the Christian faith because it proceeded from a materialistic base. That is to say, the basic assumption was that the universe is a self-contained system comprised of tiny, indivisible and indestructable atoms interacting within an infinite void of empty space. All spiritual and mental values and realities were held to be explainable strictly in terms of the interaction of these atoms. No reference to God was necessary, since the universe was self-explanatory. All that was needed for an exhaustive understanding of the universe was complete knowledge of the position and velocity of each atom at any given time. From this knowledge one could, in theory, deduce all previous and yet-to-be positions and permutations of atomistic interaction.

In our century, this interpretation of the fundamentals of physical reality has been completely overturned. With the development of Einstein's theory of relativity and Max Plank's theory of quantum mechanics, it is now most fruitful to think of a vastly complex subatomic dimension of reality that is comprised not of tiny material particles but of groupings of various points and waves of energy. Matter turns out to be highly organized and intense energy which cannot, in principle, be exhaustively known and predicted. According to Heisenberg's principle of indeterminacy, all readings taken of the velocity and/or position of any configuration of this energy will necessarily alter it, due to the fact that such readings must be taken with some energy source, such as light rays, which itself participates in and contributes to the configurations in question.

Although some scientists still insist that this more contemporary account of the fundamentals of the universe has no need of nor room for any reference to a spiritual dimension of reality, there is an increasing number of thinkers who in one way or another are interested in or are affirming the spiritual nature and importance of what is called the "new physics." At the very least, it is safe to say that physical scientists are currently exhibiting a great deal more humility in what they say about the basic nature of things and are generally more open to the possible interconnections between science and religion.

On the theological side things have changed as well. In

previous centuries nearly all theologians were content to defend Christian faith against materialism either by affirming a
spiritual realm that exists parallel to the physical (a kind of
metaphysical dualism) or by adopting an idealist philosophy
(such as classical Platonism) and denying the ultimate reality
of the material world. In light of present developments in
physics and chemistry, however, there is now a great deal of
interest in exploring the possibility of a more unified, non-
dualistic interpretation of the universe, one that sees the
material and the spiritual as different aspects of the same
reality.[3]

The two main forms this new interest is taking are (1) that
which develops the insights of the "process philosophy" of
Alfred North Whitehead and (2) that which draws heavily
upon Oriental thought, especially Buddhism and Taoism.
Whitehead suggested that reality is best understood as a vast
array of relational interactions of energy undergoing change
and growth. Out of these interactions arise the intersections
("actual occasions"), groupings ("nexus"), and federations
("societies") that we call minerals, vegetables, animals, and
minds. There is a vectorial structure of complexity and direction to these patterns of reality such that a reductionist explanation of their development will not suffice to account for
them. Whitehead, and those who follow his lead, saw his
philosophy as a way of integrating twentieth-century science
and spiritual concerns, and he affirmed the reality of a divine
being, though in somewhat unconventional terms.

Those who draw upon Eastern philosophy have been particularly interested in maintaining the importance of energy
as the center of all reality. This energy can take mental or
physical form and can be studied either according to the cate-
gories of natural science or according to those of mind and/
or spirit. These two sides or aspects of reality, experience,
and knowledge are equally important and exist in an ever-
developing process of interaction (the Yin and the Yang).
They cannot be said to exist or to be understood apart from
each other, much as the poles of an electromagnetic field
cannot exist or be studied outside of their mutual reality.

They are completely symbiotic. It is possible, given this approach, to develop some interesting and valuable ideas about God and the nature of divine involvement in the world.

Both the Whiteheadian and the Eastern interpretations of the relationship between physical and spiritual reality stress the creative interaction of God and make room for the notion of Christ as the "cosmic center" of the universe similar to that developed by Paul in his letters to the Colossians, Philippians, and Ephesians. Both these approaches imply some sense of order, direction, and/or purpose to the universe, in keeping with the fundamental themes of Judeo-Christian theism. At the same time, however, it must be acknowledged that it is this very notion of purpose or teleology in the universe that creates yet another level of difficulty in the ongoing dialogue between science and religion. It is time to take a brief look at this issue.

The question of the viability of teleological talk in science has always been a concern in the biological sciences. At least from the time of Aristotle it became customary to speak of nature as having a purpose, of the various forms of life behaving purposefully and striving to fulfill specific functions. In modern times, especially since Darwin, there has been a continuous effort to eliminate such vocabulary from scientific explanations on the grounds that these anthropomorphic "projections" are both inappropriate and unnecessary to account for biological behavior patterns. Here, again, the underlying presupposition is that nature should be explainable on its own terms, without reference to such unobservable mysteries as "intentions," "goals," and "decisions." This presupposition is part and parcel of a general commitment to limiting the scientific enterprise to those phenomena that can be objectively observed, measured, and replicated.

The concern with this issue was part of the motivation behind the search for a built-in chemical structure that would explain consistent and seemingly purposive behavior patterns. This search led from the study of genes and chromosomes to the discovery of the DNA and RNA molecular structures which transmit what used to be called "instincts" and "behavioral characteristics" from one generation of species of life to another. Some scientists claim, or at least hope, that this line of research will lead to a final explanation of all life forms, including that of humankind. The possibilities of "creating" life in a test tube and of "cloning" or manufacturing multiple, identical copies of the same person are related to this line of theorizing. On the one hand, it must be borne in mind that such complete explanations and phenomena are very far indeed from being a reality. On the other hand, skeptics, especially persons of faith, must be careful not to pontificate about what can and cannot be done by science. We must wait and see.

While we are waiting, however, we can give attention to one or two of the interesting issues that flow out of this discussion. One pertains to the question of responsibility with respect to behavior, especially that of humans. The specifics of this debate will have to wait until the next chapter, but the general consideration of determinism in nature can be hinted at here. Some religious thinkers think that the idea of a universe that is completely controlled by and predictable on the basis of previous causal factors negates entirely the possibility of a creative and loving God. Others, usually of a more Reformed or Calvinist persuasion, not only find such an approach acceptable but see it as essential to a proper understanding of the reality and sovereignty of God. For my part, I find creativity and freedom, as well as relational love and responsibility, to be at once essential to the Christian world view and incompatible with a deterministic one.

It is still possible, however, to maintain God's active and powerful involvement in the world, and the reality of divine foreknowledge, without affirming theological determinism. It is quite possible to have knowledge of how events will develop, of how beings will choose, without thereby determining or controlling them. The concepts of foreknowledge and causal determinacy are not synonymous. Moreover, Heisenberg's principle of indeterminacy establishes that the very notion of human knowledge *entails* an involvement with the nature of reality which can in no way be isolated from it. Thus, to be in the world, to interact with it, is to be part of it in such a way as to render the idea of complete causal knowledge and determinism at best useless and at worst impossible.

One other issue bearing on this general topic concerns the hierarchical nature of explanations. It is frequently assumed that the sciences are related to one another according to a hierarchy based on size. That is, that biology is reducible to physics (organic to inorganic), and that physics is reducible to chemistry (atomic to subatomic). Often this reductionistic hierarchy is extended upward, as well, so as to seek to explain psychology on the basis of biology, political science on sociology, and so on. This dimension of the problem will be treated in the next chapter. Such reductionism at the natural science level would seem to be compatible with Christian theism, especially that of a Calvinistic bent.

At the same time, however, there is an inherent difficulty with this view of the relationship among the sciences that bears mentioning.[4] The reductionistic account faces a logical difficulty when attempting to explain emergence. For the phenomenon of stratification that exists among the levels of physical reality is based, at least *prima facie*, on a qualitative distinction rather than a quantitative one. As we know it today, chemistry cannot explain and predict the phenomena classified under physics, namely the behavior of material bodies in space and time. In like manner, physics can neither explain nor predict the behavior of biological entities, because the principles of the higher or more complex level have not, and many argue *cannot*, be explained in terms of those of the less complex level. Each higher level of behavior witnesses to the emergence of a new, qualitatively distinct form of nature.

Let me illustrate at yet a higher level of complexity, one with which we are all more familiar. The fundamentals of telling time, for instance, while necessarily based on the principles of physical measurements of movement in space, are not reducible to these rules for the simple reason that "telling time" is not a concept *within* the science of physics. It is, rather, a concept *used* by but unexplained by physics. In the same way, an exhaustive knowledge of the physical principles involved in basketball will not enable one to understand the game itself, because the concepts involved in the game are not assumable under those of physics. The latter can be said to be necessary to but not sufficient for the explanation of the former. While this point may or may not be crucial to a consideration of the natural sciences, it plays a central role in the discussion of the social sciences and the humanities in the next two chapters.

Miracles And Models

One of the more popular, and still one of the more difficult, areas of debate between scientists and religious thinkers has always been that of miracles.[5] The discussion can be divided into two aspects: the *possibility* of miracles and the *actuality* of miracles. The central issue in each case traditionally revolves around the distinction between the natural order and a supernatural order. The question of possibility pertains to whether or not *any* event can be said to have an extranatural or supernatural cause, while the question of actuality pertains to whether or not a specific event can be said to in fact have a supernatural cause—assuming, of course, that an affirmative answer was given to the first question.

The general case raised against the possibility of supernatural causation is twofold. First, it is often suggested that since by definition a miracle is a violation of the laws of nature, no such event could take place. However, since the so-called "laws" of nature are nothing more than human generalized *descriptions* of the patterns nature follows, a miracle is not ruled out by definition. On the other hand, since these generalized descriptions can be said to hold with an ever-increasing degree of probability, it would seem to follow that a miracle would be highly unlikely. Moreover, since as rational creatures our beliefs should be based on the best possible evidence, it follows that we should never believe in miracles because they are by definition improbable.

Two replies to this first phase of the case against miracles can be made.[6] To begin with, since scientists are continually postulating ever more comprehensive theories and laws, perhaps it is possible to think of miracles as events expressing yet higher but still undiscovered laws of nature, rather than as violating the ones we now know. Secondly, and perhaps more importantly, it must be noted that the degree of probability of an event does not, in the final analysis, settle its actuality. Many highly improbable events do actually occur, and it will hardly do for people to object that they *could not* have occurred *because* they were improbable. Whether or not a given event has occurred must be established on the basis of evidence including but going beyond antecedent probabilities.

The second tack taken by those objecting to the very possibility of miracles is based on the meaning of scientific knowledge itself. It is argued that if the notion of miracles is allowed there can be no such thing as science, since the latter depends upon the assumption of the uniformity of nature. In other words, if it is possible for nature's basic patterns to be interrupted, then it becomes impossible to establish any causal inferences and general laws, since one would never know when a miracle would be in operation. Besides, how would we tell the difference between a supernatural event and a simple freak of nature? In short, the notion of miracle opens the door to scientific chaos, which means no science at all.

In reply to all this it is helpful to be reminded that the concept of miracle is not derived from the Judeo-Christian Scriptures. The Bible does not speak of miracles or laws of nature, but rather of God as the one who orders nature and is active in all events. The most common biblical terms are "mighty acts" (extraordinary as distinguished from ordinary events) and "signs" (vehicles of divine significance). The notion of miracles as violations of the laws of nature is a modern, intellectual one, developed by religious thinkers influenced by Greek philosophers and scientific investigations. This is not to say that it is a useless or false notion, but it is to say that perhaps the whole question of the possibility of miracles needs to be restructured. This need, along with that of addressing the reductionism inherent in much scientific reasoning, will be treated more directly in chapter 7.

The second part of the issue of miracles, whether any are *actual* (once again, assuming that a positive answer can be worked out for the first part of the issue), focuses on the nature and reliability of the evidence involved. Those who stand on the skeptical side of this question are often too quick to scoff at such claims, implying that they can never be verified, while those on the believer's side are frequently too quick to accept such claims, fearful of attempting to limit God. It would seem that the cosmos is huge and strange enough to warrant a large degree of humility on the one hand, and on the other hand it should be remembered that it does not necessarily honor God to attribute every possibility to divine intervention. Just because God *could* do anything, it does not follow that God *did* do whatever is in question. One simply must try to reflect honestly on all of the factors involved and remain open.

It must be acknowledged that a large number of claims to direct divine involvement can be explained in other ways, thereby injecting a note of caution into every such case. There are, after all, many charlatans, psychosomatic diseases, telepathic possibilities, and as yet uncharted powers and phenomena in our world. At the same time, it must be admitted that for whatever reason there are many instances of people being unexplainably healed or aided. It is difficult, if not impossible, to construct an interpretation of such happenings that will explain them all. Perhaps the most important point to be kept in mind in this inevitably confusing discussion is that having a system of interpretation that explains *everything* is neither possible nor necessary. Faith must not be equated with being able to believe certain things *in spite* of the evidence. Nor is it to be defined in terms being able to make everything fit into a preconceived theological framework. In my understanding, faith is an open-minded trusting in the *sufficiency* of the totality of our experience, a trusting that is neither defensive nor gullible.[7]

One final consideration before moving on to the social sciences. Many theologians have developed interesting and helpful ways of dealing with the notion of miracle. For instance, some have suggested that while it may be possible and necessary to view all miraculous events (such as the Israelites' escape from the Egyptians through the Reed Sea) as conforming to natural laws (winds, tides, and such), it is the particular *timing* of these events that reveals God's special activity. Thus God is viewed as working in and through natural phenomena, rather than as interrupting it.

Other theologians propose that we think of miracles as out of the ordinary, but nonetheless natural events, which take on or carry with them special religious significance for the believer or believing community. Thus, being unusual would be a necessary but not a sufficient condition for calling an event a miracle. Of particular importance to this view is the point about the event in question being discerned as bearing special significance *within* a believing community. In other words, miracles, like all religious realities, are fundamentally social in character. They are not private "viewings," nor do they take place in a corner. God's mighty acts in human history, if they mean anything, mean that the divine is active in a concrete and public fashion for redemptive purposes.

Yet other religious thinkers maintain that whereas miracles, in whatever sense, may have been God's means of interacting with the believing community in days gone by (some limit this activity to biblical times), God no longer uses such a method in modern times. It is suggested that in a time when the world view accepted and called for astounding deeds as proof of the divine, it was appropriate that God be experienced through this mode. However, now that we live in scientific times and have other explanations for such things, this mode is no longer fitting. Just as children frequently view many of the things their parents do as unexplainable "magic," but grow out of this when they mature (thereby deepening their relationship with their parents rather than weakening it), so we, too, as a result of progressive revelation have grown beyond the need of miracles, without in any way "thinning" our faith. A more subjectivist way of putting this view is to say that whenever and wherever religious communities make use of this concept, there and then the concept is viable—and where and when not, then it is not viable.

My own approach to this issue, and to the others raised in this chapter as well, is to suggest that the whole natural/ supernatural distinction be set aside in favor of an understanding of experienced reality as a hierarchy of mediated dimensions rather than as dualistic realms. God's basic relationship to the world is more *in and through* it than from above, below, or behind it. But this will have to wait until chapter 7 for a more thorough presentation. Let me conclude this chapter with a brief word about the theoretical character of science in general and its implications for theological understanding. Since these remarks apply equally well to the social sciences, perhaps they will serve as a bridge to the next chapter.

It is often thought that science deals with hard facts, not theoretical abstractions. Theology, on the other hand, is generally thought to be a highly abstract discipline. As was pointed out earlier, however, there are no facts apart from some theoretical framework, some set of concepts and procedures that render observation, inference, and experimentation possible. Moreover, these theoretic frameworks themselves are generated by and revolve around certain key concepts and metaphors, generally termed "models," that determine their character and direction.[8] These models, in turn, are not definable from within the framework, nor are they verifiable in terms of it. During certain periods within any particular science, those who work in the field do so on the basis of certain models of the world and of their procedures which are generally unarticulated. At specific junctures, say the shift from the Ptolemaic to the Copernican view of the solar system or the shift from the Newtonian to the Einsteinian view of the universe, one model is exchanged for another.[9]

This way of looking at scientific activity not only does greater justice to the way scientists work, but it also suggests many parallels to, and points of overlap between, science and theology. Theological activity, after all, is also based on and orbits around certain key notions and metaphors pertaining to the nature of divine reality, human life, and the relation between the two.[10] Not only is it helpful to explore the similarities and differences between the major world religions in terms of what might be called their "root metaphors", but even the theological differences within the Christian faith become especially meaningful when approached in this way. Whether God is viewed as a king or a friend, as a male or a female, as a force or a person, is a matter of which metaphors seem most appropriate to our experience. Indeed, the metaphors through which we are taught to view religious reality will to a large degree determine the reality we experience.

On this more fundamental, abstract level science and theology are seen to have a great deal in common, as well as a great deal to learn from each other. They both have an initial grounding in experience that sparks a behavioral and intellectual response. This response, in turn, gives rise to axial models that guide our living, thinking, and speaking. Our ongoing experience provides the confirmation or disconfirmation of these models, suggesting modifications, supplementations, and substitutions. The relationship between experience and thought, in both science and theology, is essentially circular or reciprocal in that the dynamic of living necessitates functioning on every level at once, without an actual beginning as such. We are continuously interacting, experiencing, reflecting, observing, responding, rereflecting, and so on. Both science and religion, as well as art, politics, and other enterprises, are viable and valuable modes of human activity within the world created by God. They need and complement each other, and need not—should not—be conceived of as enemies.

Suggested Reading

Barbour, Ian. *Issues in Science and Religion*. Englewood Cliffs, NJ: Prentice-Hall, 1966.

Dillenberger, John. *Protestant Thought and Natural Science*. Garden City, NY: Doubleday, 1960.

Grant, Robert. *A Short History of the Interpretation of the Bible*. New York: Macmillan, 1963.

Ramm, Bernard. *The Christian View of Science and the Scriptures*. Grand Rapids: Eerdmans, 1955.

Social Science: 3
Relativism

ON THE SURFACE, the social sciences would seem to be quite different from the natural sciences, and thus to raise quite distinct questions for religious belief. In part this is true, since the social sciences are concerned with knowledge about human beings in their psychosocial and political behavior patterns and relationships. Thus, the focus here is much more on values and responsibilities, as well as on methodological considerations. At a deeper level, however, many of the issues turn out to be similar to those raised in the previous chapter. This is especially true with respect to the question of *reductionism*. For in the social sciences as well there is a tendency to explain any given level of human life in terms of the principles inherent within the level just below it. There are even those who see social sciences as reducible to the natural sciences, from biology down to chemistry.

The other major issue that arises for those interested in the implications of the social sciences for religious belief is that of *relativism*. The Enlightenment of the eighteenth century insisted that the proper study for humankind is humankind itself, and beginning with the work of Auguste Comte in the nineteenth century, this study took a scientific turn. With the birth of sociology and anthropology, and the parallel development of psychology, the social sciences began indeed to study human behavior and activity. The major thing they were struck with was how *different* human beings are from each other, both as individuals and as groups. This observation has led in one way or another to one of the main dogmas of the twentieth century, namely relativism. Thus the social sciences revolve around reductionism and relativism, two tendencies which may well be in conflict with each other. But that is to anticipate.

BEHAVIORISM AND BENEATH

Behaviorism arose as an approach to the study of individual human life in response to two other, more subjective approaches. One was that of compiling impressionistic reports given by subjects themselves and the other was that of Freudian psychoanalysis. The desire was to establish psychology as an objective science based strictly an observable behavior without any reference to so-called mental phenomena, such as "intentions" and "motives," or "the ego" and "the subconscious." As a methodological proposal, this approach has a good deal of merit, though questions can be raised about the possibility that it systematically excludes important aspects of human life. The real difficulties arise, however, when behaviorism is expounded as a philosophical system and claims that all human life is *totally* reducible to or explainable in terms of observable behavior. This is the position advocated by B.F. Skinner and his followers.[1] Such a claim stands in need of a great deal of elaboration and substantiation.

The implications of such an understanding of human nature for religious belief are, to say the least, considerable. If observable behavior is all that can be *known* about human beings because it is all there *is*, then it becomes difficult to know how to understand the meaning of standard religious concepts such as faith, revelation, and spirit. Also, such notions as hypocrisy, conversion, and prayer would seem to be reduced to mere external rituals. Moreover, the whole question of moral responsibility becomes extremely clouded by the attempt to explain all behavior as a result of previous operant conditioning processes. Are ethical and religious ac-

tivity strictly a function of receiving certain positive reinforcements, without any basis in commitment and grace?

Many objections have been raised against behaviorism as
an approach to the study of human life. Most of them can be
organized under two main headings, namely those that pertain to epistemological issues and those that pertain to moral
issues. The former center around the possibility of knowledge and truth within a system of thought that explains *all*
human activity, including theorizing about human behavior
(as with behaviorism) as a result of conditioning processes.
For, if this view is itself advanced as true, then it, too—as well
as believing it—turns out to be nothing more than the out-
come of a particular conditioning process. In short, what the
theory *claims* completely undercuts the possibility of *affirming*
it, since all behavior, including affirmations and denials, is
reduced to the same logical level, namely conditioned response. The concepts of "truth" and "falsehood" no longer
have any meaning.

Consider the following example. Suppose someone says
that he or she objects to Skinner's theory, not on the grounds
that it is empirically false or logically unsound, but because
this person simply has not as yet received "sufficient positive
reinforcement"? Skinner can only reply that the person must
reconsider his data, arguments, and so on; but according to
his own theory these concepts have no other meaning than
that they are forms of reinforcement which certain individuals (the members of the scientific community) respond to
positively. There is no logical difference between scientific
data and a handful of jellybeans if they both bring about the
desired results, namely acceptance. In fact, Skinner's own affirmation of his theory turns out to be nothing but certain
verbal behavior that has been positively reinforced. He does
not believe it because he has been "convinced" of its truth by
the evidence. Rather, he accepts it because he has been *conditioned* to do so!

Thus, it is possible to respond to the claim that religious
belief is "nothing but" behavior which has been conditioned
by positive reinforcement. The appropriate response is that *if*

Skinner is right, then *all* behavior—including belief in behav-iorism—is "nothing but" conditioning. In fact, the very meaning of being "right" is lost, since accepting something as right only differs from not doing so by having received suffi-cient positive reinforcement. In a word, the very possibility of truth, indeed of meaningful language, is undercut by philo-sophical behaviorism. As a challenge to religious belief it fails because it proves too much, hoisting itself with its own pe-tard.

The second main body of objections to behaviorism cluster around the issues of freedom and responsibility. According to behaviorism, these concepts cannot be said to have mean-ing in their traditional usage because they are generally taken to refer to some internal, unobservable mental or volitional reality that supposedly forms the basis of our behavior. In reality, however, our behavior is not only all that can be known scientifically, but it is all that can be meant by such terms. We *are* our behavior, period. Thus, the notions em-ployed when we speak about moral choices and responsibil-ity must be understood as making reference to various modes of observable behavior, not to private, internal realities. This claim, in itself, may not pose any substantial difficulty for those involved and interested in religious ethics. In fact, some actually welcome the shift in emphasis from internal, "pietis-tic privatism" to external, social involvement as the crux of Christian morality. After all, it was Jesus who said, "By their fruits you shall know them."

The serious difficulties arise when the causal implications of behaviorism are followed up. For now it becomes clear that according to this view, all of our moral choices and ac-tivities, now understood as behavior, are *entirely* the result of previous conditioning processes. We do not "choose" our moral commitments and involvements in the traditional way of understanding this term. Rather, our choices are simply behavioral responses that have received sufficient positive re-inforcement to cause us to continue in them. In other words, beneath behaviorism lies the presupposition of complete causal determinism. Although this may not be problematic for religious people who are willing to accept the strong version of Reformed theology in which it is affirmed that God is the ultimate cause of every event that transpires in the universe, it is highly problematic for those who affirm the crucial nature of free choice and individual responsibility to meaningful religious faith.

One move that can be made in response to this aspect of behaviorism is to point out that once again it has caught itself up in its own trap. For Skinner and other behaviorists are *urging* the rest of us to *choose* or accept the behaviorist account of moral choice as true, and supposedly they themselves have chosen to accept it as such. But what meaning does the concept of choice have if, in fact, behaviorism is true? It would seem that all choices are merely effects in a long line of causal determinants. The irony of the behaviorist position with respect to morality is especially sharp in Skinner's book, *Beyond Freedom and Dignity,* where he argues in favor of, and urges us to accept the responsibility for, a view of human nature (i.e., behaviorism) that defines such concepts as freedom and responsibility strictly in terms of operant conditioning. Skinner affirms that this is not only the *true* (!) view, but the only one that will enable us to *control* and take *responsibility* for our own future. He urges us to choose those conditioning processes that will enable our species to survive. Such urgings contradict what is being urged.

Another move that can be made here is to point out that there remains, even within the behaviorist account, an important distinction between *causes* and *reasons*. Human behavior can be understood in terms of causal determinants, as part of the causal network governing the physical universe. But it can also be understood, and is generally so understood (even within behaviorism!) in terms of reasons and choices. Behaviorists themselves give reasons for accepting the behaviorist point of view and they *choose* to accept these *reasons*, as has been pointed out in the foregoing paragraphs.

Some thinkers argue that these two modes of thinking and

speaking are mutually compatible and coextensive. That is, they both cover exactly the same phenomena, each from its own perspective, without in any way conflicting with each other. It is maintained that when doing science we study the causal network and when engaged in ethical discussions we employ the language of reasons and intentions. There is, of course, a problem when these two realms of discourse seem to overlap, as in legal contexts, when both languages are deemed relevant. The recent flap about the viability of insanity pleas clearly illustrates this difficulty. It would seem that some way has to be developed to work out the intricacies of such overlaps, or at least of establishing a system of priorities with respect to the two modes of thought.

My own inclination is to suggest that the mode of discourse involving reasons is, in fact, more basic to all human life and activity than any other, including that mode involving causal judgments. Although the latter is itself exceedingly crucial, it is predicted on the assumption that there is an essential difference between rational choice and conditioning, and between truth and falsehood, a difference which cannot be set aside without undermining the whole scientific enterprise. The logical priority of rational discourse, in the sense of giving reasons as a basis for decisions and choices, is graphically clear in Skinner's own writing. He continually appeals to logic and evidence, not other reinforcements, by way of influencing the reader's judgment. This is also true with respect to the priority of rational discourse in the realm of moral responsibility. Our commitment, and Skinner's as well, to the morality of truth-telling and responsible belief is what undergirds our search for causal connections and conditioning processes. Both our verbal and nonverbal behavior make this abundantly clear.

Interesting light is cast upon this whole issue, and substantiation of the above position is provided, by the insight that talk of causal factors in relation to responsibility questions only becomes relevant in the uncommon situation, when the usual ways of speaking break down. For instance, an action may be explained and responsibility removed when it is made clear that the subject was forced at gunpoint to drive the getaway car, or was functioning under great emotional strain due to a recent traumatic experience, or was bumped from behind, and so on. In the absence of such mitigating circumstances, it is assumed that people are responsible for their deeds *because* it is presumed that they are free. Moral and rational freedom are the preconditions of all responsible human behavior. Thus, in my view the basis of religious faith as a responsible commitment, together with moral responsibility within the context of Christian ethics, is in no way threatened by the reductionism inherent in behaviorism.

OBJECTIVISM AND HISTORICISM

Two of the primary characteristics of the contemporary concern to establish the social sciences as sciences *par excellence* are a commitment to *objectivity* on the one hand and espousement of historical and cultural *relativity* on the other hand. The obvious tension that naturally arises between these two commitments constitutes the drama of this particular phase of humankind's search for knowledge of social reality. The concern to be as objective as possible in all observations and inferences entails the presupposition that there is an absolute, nonperspectival account of reality toward which we are steadily progressing. At the same time, however, the acknowledgment of the integrity of each historical and/or cultural context in determining its own truth entails the conclusion that all truth is relative to the perspective of the observer(s).

For some, the implications of objectivism are not all problematic with respect to the viability of religious faith. In fact, they would see such an account of truth fundamental to Christian theistic belief, for it goes hand in hand with the belief that God's perspective on reality is an absolute one, that God's truth is the truth. Of course, it is possible to admit that God's view of reality constitutes absolute truth, while yet maintaining that no human view will ever reflect God's truth fully, and thus such an absolute perspective is irrelevant to our epistemological endeavors. In fact, some would argue that to fail to acknowledge the necessary relativity of *any* and *every* human perspective is the primary cause of theological confusion and difficulty, as even a cursory reading of the history of the church will substantiate.

There are at least two serious philosophical critiques of objectivism that have particular relevance for our knowledge of social reality. The first[2] pertains to the fact that such knowledge is *our* knowledge in the sense that the very concepts and activities which comprise social knowledge (which are its preconditions) are themselves part and parcel of the reality being studied. We can only make sense of those forms of behavior which we recognize as such because we participate in them ourselves. Moreover, the activities of making observations and inferences, the very heart of the scientific method, are themselves *social* activities and as such are an important aspect of social reality. Thus the "sociology of knowledge" raises problems for objectivism by suggesting that all human knowledge is the result of human processes and notions, thereby eliminating the possibility of an absolute perspective.

Another way to put this point is the following:[3] All knowing takes place within some cultural and intellectual framework. Outside of a previously agreed upon set of concepts and activities there are no such things as "facts" and "truths." In short, all facts are "theory-laden," they all entail a theoretical framework of some sort. Some thinkers[4] would go so far as to argue that we *create* our worlds as well as the facts within them, that our very ways of coming at the world (scientific, religious, aesthetic, economic, etc.) are the result of different "fashioning procedures" that we adopt for various common purposes. The upshot of this line of reasoning is that all epistemological considerations themselves must take place within a theoretic structure of some sort, and thus the notion of an absolute, completely objective perspective simply makes no sense.

The second philosophical criticism of objectivism is directed more at the personal level of epistemological activity.[5] The point here is that whenever we make a knowledge claim we are implicitly accrediting our own powers of observation and judgment, we are affirming that we take responsibility for the reliability of our claim, and we give to others the right to rely on our judgment. Every effort to divest our epistmological enterprise of this personal dimension is doomed from the outset because any such move must be made by an individual knower who takes responsibility for his or her claim—including the claim that human knowledge can transcend the personal level. Knowledge may be more than individual commitment, but it is never less. Thus an absolutist perspective is out of the question.

In my opinion, there is a great deal of force to these criticisms of objectivism. I believe that modern philosophy and science have taken a good thing too far, that they have virtually made a cult out of objectivity. It is one thing to seek to overcome individual and cultural bias by stressing the need for public discussion and confirmation. It is quite another to talk as if absolute truth, devoid of human "contamination" is possible for human knowers. At the same time, there certainly seems to be value in seeking to get beyond each and every perspective that is developed. Granting that all knowledge is relative to time, place, and persons, some perspectives seem to be "better" than others, at least for certain purposes, and in some sense these must be "more" true, or closer to *the* truth. This would seem to apply to religious claims as well.

One move that I find helpful in this situation is to suggest that perhaps it is possible to speak and think of the absolute perspective, or "objective truth," as a kind of abstract, regulative notion whose only function is to remind us never to be satisfied with *any* human perspective as the final truth. This has specific ramifications for theological claims to truth, especially as they bear on our understanding of human nature and development. The history of theological judgments in the fields comprising the social sciences is not much better than in the natural sciences. The opinions of religious bodies and individuals about personality, cultural developments, and socioeconomic policies are always appropriate, and occasionally even helpful, but when they claim to speak with finality and objective authority they go too far. A commitment to an absolute truth, in principle only, actually serves to chasten those who would claim to have achieved it.

All of this brings up the topic of revelation. There are those who maintain that since the Christian faith, especially the Bible, constitutes a revelation from God, it provides us with absolute truth. Admittedly, this topic is as important as it is complicated, but since this is not a book on theology as such, we can only treat it briefly here.

Aside from the fact that there are a great many subjects on which Christian revelation (or any claim to revelation, for that matter) does not speak at all, there are other difficulties which are more serious.

Perhaps the central issue here is whether or not the Christian revelation is understood as *propositional* in nature. Traditionally many theologians have taken the Bible, as originally written, as a collection of truths about God and humanity stated in propositional form (X is Y). Other, primarily contemporary thinkers, have suggested that God's revelation in the Judeo-Christian religion is always in *events*, not in propositions. The mighty *acts* of God in history, culminating in the Incarnation of Christ in Jesus, are said to constitute revelation. The Scriptures are understood as the response to, record of, and interpretation of God's revelation by the believing community.

While I myself am of the latter opinion, in the final analysis it may not matter which of these views one takes. For in either case, it is not possible to eliminate the human, interpretive element. Even if the Bible is taken as a propositional revelation from God, no propositions are self-interpreting, apart from an understanding of the languages, purposes, and historical and cultural settings involved. This was as true for the original recipients of the Scriptures, or even of visions, dreams, and so on, as it is for us today. Each person, or at least each community, has to determine for himself or herself whether or not God has actually spoken or acted, and what the meaning of this revelation is. I do not see this as giving rise to any special difficulties for the possibility of religious knowledge, since it is obvious that the Incarnation clearly involves a *mediated* concept of revelation; that is, "through a glass, darkly." We shall return to this issue in chapter 7.

The criticisms of objectivism mentioned in the foregoing discussion naturally lead, when carried to their logical extreme, to the position known as "historicism." This is the view that truth is relative to the time and space frame within which a given knower or group exists. Historians and anthropologists have given us good reason to acknowledge that often this is a valid point to keep in mind. What is accepted and counted as truth in one culture may not be in another, with respect both to morality and to factual knowledge. Even the arrogance of the Western scientific perspective, which tends to see the views and practices of other times and place as "primitive," must come under the judgment of historical and cultural relativism. As we have already seen, this posture has specific ramifications for the notion of religious knowledge, since such knowledge must be expressed in given historical and cultural forms, forms that cannot claim to transcend these common principles without being guilty of arrogance.

The limitations of historicism and cultural relativism reveal themselves, however, when the claim they make concerning the so-called "subjective" character of all knowledge is applied to this claim itself. It would certainly seem that if *all* knowledge is relative, then even the knowledge *that* all knowledge is relative must be relative—which is either circular or nonsensical. In other words, this position undercuts itself, since *what* is affirmed is contradicted by the *saying* of it. For, when a person asserts that all knowledge is relative, he or she expects this to be understood and accepted as a universal, absolute truth.

This particular self-negating paradox calls our attention
once again to the necessity of an abstract, regulative notion of
truth, one which we *intend* or aim at whenever we assert
something as true.[6] When we make a knowledge claim we
affirm our common commitment to *seek* the truth that is true
for *everyone*, even as we acknowledge that as humans we shall
never arrive at it. This concept of "universal intent" that is
operative amidst all of our epistemological activity guards
against the excesses of relativism, while our acknowledgment
of the sociality and contextuality of all human judgments
guards against the excesses of absolutism.

This twofold dynamic of our epistemological situation applies equally well to the notion of religious truth about human nature and development. God's truth may be spoken of
as absolute and objective, as that at which we aim in our
search for knowledge, even though we must always remind
ourselves that *our* knowledge of God's truth is of necessity
contextual and approximate, and thus is relative. This is
equally true of knowledge which we claim to be revealed of
God, because even *this* claim (as well as that which is said to
be revealed) must be discerned and confirmed *as* true in and
through the human situation.

The idea that there is no absolute truth available to us
through revelation is disconcerting to many. For my part I do
not find it so, and that for two reasons. First, there simply is
no way around this reality. We are who and what we are, and
all of our knowledge is just that, *ours!* But this hardly renders
us epistemologically impotent, for we have no trouble carrying on societal, scientific, and personal relationships on the
basis of such non-absolute knowledge. Second, it seems clear
that had God wished to communicate absolute knowledge to
us, it would have been done in a manner other than the way
Judeo-Christian revelation has taken place. God acted in history, in events among humans; the Word became *flesh*, not a
concept or a set of propositions. Christian revelation is *mediated* through a person in interaction with other persons, and

as such is *sufficient* without being absolute in the epistemological sense.

Here again we find that the challenge of the social sciences to religious belief, especially with respect to objectivism and historicism, to be every bit as helpful as it is threatening. For it challenges us to acknowledge the limitations of our human condition, both theologically and scientifically, without necessitating that we give up on the possibility of reliable knowledge in either.

FUNCTIONALISM AND MARXISM

The two remaining areas of interface between religious belief and the social sciences that we shall take up arise from within social theory. The first centers in sociology proper and the sociology of religion in particular. The second is based in the philosophy of history and economics. The former is especially well-focused by Emile Durkheim's theory of the origin and role of religion in society, often termed "functionalism." The latter is powerfully expressed in the theoretic formulations of Karl Marx. Both constitute a more *direct* threat to the viability of Christian faith than do those postures we have already considered, yet both have genuine contributions to make to our understanding of religious commitment.

Put quite bluntly, functionalism is the view that religion arises and continues to play a meaningful role in societies because and as long as it serves to bind people together by giving them a common mythology and modes of legitimization. Durkheim's views gave a particular sociological twist to the historicism discussed in the previous section.[7] He maintained that every culture develops its religion in accord with its distinctive needs and concerns by way of maintaining and shaping itself. Thus both religious practices *and* beliefs are valuable and viable, not because they reflect some truth about divine being in relation to human life, but because they serve a useful sociological function.

As an explanation of the origin and nature of religion, this theory offers a better account than Freud's explanation of religion, for instance, by acknowledging the positive role that religion plays rather than simply designating it an infantile and oppressive holdover from primordial tribalism. Furthermore, with respect to the ongoing value of religion in a given society, functionalism enables us to understand better the development of what some call the "post-Christian era" in our own society. There are those who argue, with more than minimal cogency, that our culture is disintegrating and that it is doing so precisely because we have ceased to believe and practice our common religious heritage. The fact that some view this development positively while others view it negatively is an extremely interesting topic that we shall not be able to pursue here.

From the perspective provided by functionalism we are enabled to feel, as well, the force of the criticisms leveled at religion in general and at Christianity in particular by those who claim that it has often served as an instrument of oppression and destruction in the hands of a few especially "chosen ones." Frequently those who have held power in a society have gained and maintained it by manipulating religious structures and events. The "priestly class" in almost every culture of subculture has exploited religion for its own ends as often as not, as a quick survey of the history of any religion will testify. In Christianity one has only to mention the Crusades, the Inquisition, the witch trials, holy wars, the enslavement of Africans in America, Nazism, and so on. These are obvious cases of people acting "in God's name" to exploit others for their own advantage. A discussion of the not-so-obvious dimensions of this phenomenon would be worthwhile but not central to our present purposes.

Another positive aspect of the functionalist analysis of religion is this: it reminds us that religious belief, whatever else it should be and do, should also make a contribution to the character and development of our society. Frequently Christians have failed to see that faith has as much to do with life in community and culture as it does with individual beliefs and practices. This has resulted in a strong dichotomy between the sacred and the secular, between private faith and public life in our society. We are, after all, both in creation and in redemption, social beings with responsibilities for our common life. We were created in God's image and in community, and the entire Judeo-Christian tradition is built upon the notion of the *people* of God, whether as Israel or as the body of Christ. There *is* a definite sense in which religious faith ought to serve a functional role in society.[8]

After having acknowledged the foregoing assets of functionalism, however, it is important to pay some attention to the debits. The crucial issue is, of course, whether or not one wishes to claim that religion is *exclusively* a matter of fulfilling certain needs and functions within a given society. It certainly seems legitimate, indeed necessary and valuable, to acknowledge that this is one important aspect or dimension of the meaning of religion. At the same time it seems equally certain that there is no way of establishing this as the only role religion plays, or indeed that a functional analysis is the only appropriate way of thinking about religious belief. To put it differently, *that* religion functions in a certain way does not *entail* that this is its essential nature or that this is all it does. There are, after all, individual psychological aspects of religious life, as well as aspects which deliberately focus criticisms of its established, traditional beliefs and practices.

Theologically speaking, the central concern is whether or not, given its functional role, religion reveals a divine dimension as well. It does not seem that these two are mutually exclusive. They would only be opposed to each other if they were defined as pertaining to two completely distinct realms, such as the natural and the supernatural. This is, to be sure, the way they have often been defined, but such a definition leads to such a radical dichotomy between faith and the rest of life as to be counterproductive. Besides, if the Incarnation means anything it means that God is interested in the enfleshment of spiritual reality in *this* world, in the living out of divine love in *all* of life. The Incarnation embodies the unity of the natural and the supernatural.

This incarnational way of thinking leads directly to the possibility that we can think of divine activity in the world as *mediated* in and through the natural and the social, rather than as totally transcendent to and interruptive of them. The idea here would be that the divine and the natural are related more as interpenetrating *dimensions* than as stacked realms or levels. Thus it would be both possible and helpful to think of religious reality as sociologically functional and as more than this as well. The spelling-out of this "more" is dependent upon a fuller presentation of a fresh way of thinking about experienced reality in general, and hence must once again wait until chapter 7.

Finally, a brief consideration of the Marxist understanding of religious faith will prove helpful as a way of bringing this chapter to a close.[9] In some ways, with respect to the nature of religious belief, Marxist thought serves as a special case of Durkheim's theory. Marx, too, viewed religion as fulfilling a sociological function. His particular emphasis, however, was on the negative role it plays in human life. For those who are *oppressed* it serves to keep them in their place by stressing the God-given nature of their socioeconomic status and the rewards they will receive in the next life if they submit gracefully to this status. For those who are the *oppressors* it provides legitimation of their privileged place by grounding it in the divine order of things and emphasizing their responsibility. Thus religion is the "opiate of the people."

The philosophical basis of Marx's "dialectical materialism" is found in his view of history and society. He borrowed the notion of the dialectic struggle of human development—thesis, antithesis, synthesis—from Hegel and applied it to a materialistic understanding of the division of society into classes (the "haves" and the "have-nots"). His materialism had little to do with the classical philosophical position about atoms and the void. Rather, it pertained to the necessary grounding of all human activity and understanding in the "material conditions" of human existence, namely the means of economic production and distribution. Marx maintained that the whole of human history and civilization can and must be explained in terms of the dialectical struggle among the social classes. Each particular phase of the struggle arises out of the previous and in turn gives rise to the next phase.

In this way Marxist thought comes to the conclusion that the entire "superstructure" of Western society, including the political, educational, artistic, and religious aspects, are *determined* by the dynamics of the "substructure," namely the economic system. Without going into the details of the Marxist analysis of capitalism's contribution to the escalation of the dialectical struggle to its final phase and beyond (the revolution of the oppressed and the ensuing classless society), it is easy to see the rationale for Marx's negative evaluation of religion. Not only does it serve the ruling class in its efforts to control and exploit the working class, but it is strictly a function of socioeconomic determinants as well. That is to say, the Marxist religion is nothing more than what the material conditions of society make it to be. All reference to any reality beyond the natural and the human is set aside.

As was the case with Durkheim's functionalism, so with Marxist materialism. Everything depends on how strongly one takes the key thesis, namely that the entire superstructure is a *function* of the substructure. If this is taken in the strongest sense, then Marxism must be read as denying all possibility of synthesis with standard religious belief, and thus in spite of its many insights into the shortcomings of traditional religion and capitalist society, it is in direct conflict with Christian faith. On the other hand, if this form of functionalism can be taken to mean that to a *large degree* and in a specifically *sociological* sense religion, along with the other aspects of culture, is dependent on the economic structure, then there remains room for some form of integration of Marxism and religious belief.

There are, in fact, interpreters of Marx who read him in this latter way,[10] and thus take him as a humanist who need not have been as opposed to religion as he is usually made out to have been. Moreover, there are theologians who have made and continue to make powerful use of the Marxist understanding of human nature and society in their development of Christian theology and social ethics.[11] Once again we find ourselves in need of an understanding of the nature of the relation between the divine and the human which, unlike the traditional, dualistic way of thinking, will enable us to integrate the two dimensions of reality without trivializing either. An introductory presentation of such an understanding is the burden of chapter 7. But that must wait until our survey of the various disciplines within the academy is complete.

Suggested Reading

Bonino, José. *Doing Theology in a Revolutionary Situation*. Philadelphia: Fortress, 1975.

Cox, Harvey. *The Secular City*. (New York: Macmillan, 1965).

Shaull, Richard. *Containment and Change*. New York: Macmillan, 1967.

Stevenson, Leslie. *Seven Theories of Human Nature*. New York: Oxford Univ. Press, 1974.

West, Charles. *Communism and The Theologians*. New York: Macmillan, 1963.

The Humanities: 4
Humanism

By the humanities I mean those disciplines that traditionally fall under the heading, "History of Ideas." This includes especially philosophy, religion, and literature. There are, to be sure, other fields that border on or overlap these, such as history, psychology, and social theory (depending on how they are pursued), but generally these are thought of today as scientific endeavors. My intention is not to exclude but simply to provide focus by centering the following discussion on philosophy broadly conceived. The arts will receive their due in the next chapter. Once again it should be mentioned that our concern is to trace and engage in dialogue the main developments in these fields as they bear on the nature and meaning of Christian faith.

The Vertical and the Horizontal

Broadly speaking, the history of ideas in the West divides into two main periods, which for lack of better terms I shall call the "Classical" and the "Modern." The former includes everything from the ancient Hebrews and their contemporaries (with some notable exceptions), through ancient Greece and Rome, to what we call the Medieval age, Augustine through Aquinas especially. The latter started around 1500, with the discovery of the Americas, the Reformation, the Renaissance, and the ascendancy of the scientific method.

It begins with the Rationalists (Descartes and Spinoza) and early Empiricists (Francis Bacon and Thomas Hobbes), continues on through the Enlightment (David Hume and Immanuel Kant) and various nineteenth-century responses to it (Hegel, Nietzsche, Marx, Kierkegaard), and leads us midway into the present century, dominated by Positivism (Russell, Wittgenstein, Carnap) and Existentialism (Sartre, Camus, Heidegger).

At the risk of oversimplification, I suggest that the fundamental difference between the Classical and Modern periods of Western thought has to do with a shift from thinking of reality as two-dimensional to thinking of it as one-dimensional. The Classical period theorized about reality in terms of both a vertical dimension (the transcendent) and a horizontal dimension (the natural and the human). The Modern period has been characterized by the *denial* of the reality, or at least of the relevance, of the vertical and the *affirmation* of the exclusive, or at least the sufficient, reality of the horizontal. In other words, the Modern way of theorizing about the world and human existence claims to have no need of any transcendent dimension whatsoever. Indeed, references to vertical aspects of reality are generally considered to be more harmful than helpful. The natural and human horizontal dimension is considered quite adequate to account for the nature and meaning of both the world and human experience.

The primary features of the Classical understanding were three. To begin with, there was the belief that reality is comprised of *two main realms*, the natural and the transcendent. In Greek thought this view was most forcefully articulated by Plato's theory of Forms, according to which the reality of this lower world is explained and understood as a "reflection" or representation of the higher, abstract world of concepts or ideas. The latter were said to be eternal and unchanging, while the constituents of the former world were viewed as transitory and unreliable.

Secondly, this *metaphysical* dualism was paralled by an *epistemological* dualism that expressed itself in the contrast between the body and the mind (the "eye of the soul"). Plato and his followers, which in one way or another included nearly everyone for centuries to come, maintained that through the body we live in and know this world while through the mind we know and come to participate in the transcendent world of ideas. The suggestion was that the goal of life is to transcend the body ("the prisonhouse of the soul") and live in a world of Forms by developing our rational capacities.

This twofold dualism was adopted and adapted by early Christian thinkers, such as Augustine, as the most helpful way to give theological expression to the teachings of the Judeo-Christian Scriptures. Thus the world of the Forms was paralleled to (even occasionally identified with) the heavenly realm, the ultimate home of the soul, while the material world (and especially the body) was paralleled to the fallen, sinful state of humanity. The proper relationship of the soul with its Creator, through Christ, was, of course, substituted for the development of human rational capacities as the mode of salvation.

Thirdly, a word more about this salvation process. According to Classical philosophy, the root metaphor on which knowledge of the Forms was based was that of *vision*. The soul was likened to the eye and truth was defined as seeing the realm of beauty and goodness clearly by means of logical reasoning. In like manner, in Christian thought, salvation has traditionally been understood as the soul's clear vision of God and the heavenly realm, made possible by faith in Christ's revelatory and redemptive work. Error, or sin, on the other hand, was defined as distorted vision or blindness that hinders or eliminates one's understanding. We shall return to the crucial nature of this metaphor in chapter 7.

Beginning with the early rationalists and empiricists, the above understanding of reality began to recede. More and more it became possible and perhaps advisable to seek ways of explaining the nature and meaning of the world and human life strictly on the basis of principles inherent within this realm. Whether our knowledge of reality was said to be based in rationality or experience did not really matter, since both of these are within the confines of the horizontal dimension. What needs to and can be known about the world and life is now said to be attainable apart from any reference to a higher, transcendent realm. Although some thinkers, notably of a religious bent, have continued to affirm the reality and necessity of the vertical dimension, the dominant character of the Modern age is this-worldly in nature.

The horizontal emphasis of modernity has taken two main forms. One is *naturalistic* in that it stresses the full and complete inclusion of human life within the structures and dynamics of the natural world. According to this approach, humans are in reality just another, albeit a highly complex, form of animal existence. All rationality and morality are said to be explainable entirely within the principles used to explain all other forms of material and biological reality. Often this line of thinking makes great use of evolutionary thought, stressing both our integral relation to natural processes and our opportunities to preserve and advance them.

The other main form of Modern, horizontal thought is *humanism*. In a way this approach is something of a compromise between traditional dualism and naturalism. While agreeing with naturalists that the horizontal dimension is sufficient to account for human life and values, humanists continue to affirm the uniqueness of human existence in relation to other forms of life. They generally maintain that the sphere of human values and meaning represents the highest level of the natural realm, and thus is in some sense more important than the rest of it, without in any way wishing to imply that it transcends this realm. Utilitarian thought along with various forms of humanitarianism provide the main expressions of the humanist ethical thrust.

Because of the strong parallels and interweaving between Classical theology and philosophy, most religious thinkers have felt it necessary to defend the traditional dualist view of reality, human nature, and knowledge against the claims and attacks of the Modern, one-dimensional posture. All forms of naturalism, and even humanism, are frequently thought of as the enemy of religious belief. While I can see the merits and demerits of both approaches, I think it neither necessary nor wise to choose one over the other. This is not because I propose some sort of eclectic compromise between the two, but rather because I submit that both are predicated on a common presuppositional base which must itself be disposed of before a sound and fruitful integration of the values of each approach can be worked out. Let me explain.

Although traditional dualism and modern "horizontalism" disagree about how many realms or levels there are in reality, and although this difference is extremely important, it remains true that at the most fundamental level the two approaches are in agreement. Their agreement consists in mutually assuming that reality is best understood as comprised of realms or levels. They disagree about how many levels there are, but they both take up the debate in terms of such levels without questioning this way of structuring the discussion. It is this initial assumption that must, in my opinion, be questioned and replaced by a *dimensional* model of reality, one in which the richer, more intangible dimensions are mediated in and through the less rich and more tangible dimensions. (The much-advertised chapter 7 will consist of a more thorough effort to introduce this model.)

The dualist view *does* seem to carry with it the advantage of grounding human and spiritual truth and values in such a way as to preserve their inherent and intrinsic worth against the obvious possibilities for erosion by reductionism and relativism. This clearly is more in line with the Christian understanding of truth and reality than is a one-dimensional view. At the same time, however, it must be acknowledged that this advantage comes at unduly high price. For to posit a two-story world view entails at least three serious difficulties.

First, such a view has proven itself to lead to strong dichotomies between the sacred and the secular, to become "so heavenly minded as to be of no earthly good." Second, it has always been extremely difficult to establish the reality and relevance of a realm that is essentially transcendent to this realm, since it is by definition *beyond* us. Third, this dualist approach entails viewing any revelation of the divine as an *intrusion* into the natural realm. These last two difficulties focus the problem of choosing the criteria by which to recognize a revelation of the transcendent, since the only ones available to us are those of the natural order. Being bizarre will hardly serve as a useful criterion for true revelation.

The one-dimensional or horizontalist view has the advantage of rendering this world extremely important in the scheme of things. This is an advantage, in my judgment, because the Judeo-Christian Scriptures do not in any way suggest the sort of other-worldly emphasis that traditional theological systems have affirmed. The Hebrew perspective was wisely much less dualistic than that of the Greeks, and in some respects the Modern view represents a return to it. In addition, however, the humanist or naturalist approaches *do* have difficulty establishing any solid basis for values and meaning in human life. Witness the increased breakdown of moral integrity that parallels the rise of the modern, secular understanding of life.

Moreover, there do seem to be inherent inconsistencies in a world view that both affirms the importance of rational explanation and at the same time denies that such intelligibility has any basis beyond itself.[1] The "universal intent" inherent within the drive to understand would seem to require that intelligibility itself must be integral to the nature of the cosmos. This suggests a dimension of reality that in some way transcends the human. The crucial question is, Is there any way to preserve the advantages of both these approaches while avoiding their difficulties? As I have already indicated several times, it is my contention that this can only be done by jettisoning the "realm–istic" presupposition common to both in favor of a model involving a series of mediated dimensions arranged according to a hierarchy of richness and comprehensiveness. (Chapter 7 still lies ahead!)

VERIFICATION AND MEANING

With the turn of the century, an important shift took place in the humanities, especially well-focused in philosophy. Whereas up to this point the primary concern had always been with truth and reality, in the twentieth century the stress has been placed on *meaning*. The dual foci of this fresh concern have been two movements broadly known as linguistic philosophy and existentialism. I shall sketch out the main profile of the former, together with its impact on religious belief, in this section, and that of the latter in the next section. Each movement has been exploring the concept of meaning in its own way: linguistic philosophy has emphasized the meaning of language, while existentialism has examined the meaning of individual human existence.

Some of the roots of linguistic philosophy were in Vienna (with a group known as the Vienna Circle), while others were in England, primarily in the work of Bertrand Russell and the young Ludwig Wittgenstein. The Viennese group sought to explain language and meaningfulness on the basis of what they took scientific discourse to be, while the British sought to come at it from the perspective of logic and mathematics. Both root systems received their most direct and influential expression in the book *Language, Truth, and Logic* by A.J. Ayer, a young Englishman who had studied in Vienna.[2] Just prior to World War II, many members of the Vienna Circle came to America, and after the war many American philosophers studied in England. Thus this movement came to be the dominant one this side of the Atlantic.

The central thrust of Ayer's book, as well as of early linguistic philosophy (often termed "analytic philosophy"), was the "verifiability criterion of meaningfulness." The point of this formidable sounding mouthful was really quite simple. The idea was to try to settle whether or not a statement or a theory is actually a *meaningful* one before investing a great deal of effort on the question of its truth. This resulted in proposing that unless a given proposition could in principle be checked out, *tested* as to its truth value, it would be set aside as cognitively meaningless. That is to say, unless a statement can be shown to be strictly redundant or self-contradictory (according to the laws of logic) on the one hand, or in some way reducible to propositions about concrete, observable experience on the other hand, it is simply devoid of any possible truth value (cognitivity).

An example should prove helpful at this point. Let's say I assert that the room you are now in is full of hippopotamuses. You look around and report that you do not see, hear, or smell any such animals at all. To which I reply, "Of course not—they are in principle inexperienceable hippopotamuses." Now, since I affirm that these beasts of mine are "in principle" beyond experience, it follows that there is absolutely no way to establish whether my statement is true or false. In short, it is a meaningless mouthing of sounds that appears to be affirming something but actually is not; just as the words "Why is a mouse when it whirls?" appear to be asking a question but are not. Another way to point out the meaninglessness of my utterance is to reflect on the fact that there is no difference at all between affirming it and denying it; both acts result in the same experiences. If *nothing* counts for or against a proposition, it can hardly be said to be making a cognitive claim.

Now Ayer's concern was not with hippopotamuses, but with the claims philosophers and theologians have been making for thousands of years about such notions as the eternal Forms of Truth and Beauty, a reality that entirely transcends the one we know, God and angels, our absolute duty, and the like. He proposed that we set aside all such questions as meaningless because they are in principle irresolvable, and thus are a waste of time and effort. All metaphysical, theological, and ethical statements are thus classified as *cognitively meaningless*, though they well may be *emotionally meaningful* to many people. Emotional meaning, however, was said not to be the business of philosophy, but rather that of counselors, family, and friends.

The force of this fresh challenge to those who would speak religiously was, and is, considerable. Whereas prior to this the main issue had been whether or not religious statements were true, now the issue became whether or not they are even asserting anything. In the words of the young Wittgenstein, taken from his highly influential book *Tractatus Logico-Philosophicus* (a book that powerfully informed Ayer's work): "Whatever can be said at all can be said clearly. Whereof we cannot speak, thereof we must remain silent." Talk of God was thus placed beyond the range of meaningful discourse, because there would seem to be no way to evaluate it. In a word, religious language, along with all metaphysical and ethical language, does not meet the verifiability criterion of meaningfulness.

A wide variety of responses[3] to the challenge of early linguistic, or analytic, philosophy have been made by those who find speaking religiously a valuable activity. There were those who welcomed this emphasis because it brings out what they took to be the central purpose of God-talk, namely to focus our emotive and moral perspectives. These thinkers claimed that by means of the religious use of language we express our deepest commitments. Other thinkers have argued that God-talk *is*, in fact, beyond the reach of cognitive meaning, not because it is meaningless nor because it is essentially emotive or moral in its nature, but rather because it is personal and mysterious. In other words, these thinkers maintain that religious discourse is unique, following criteria of its own, and this need not answer to those of scientific or philosophic discourse.

At the same time there were, and are, those who contend that God-talk can be shown to *meet* the verifiability criterion of meaningfulness. Some thinkers maintain that there are religious or "metaphysical facts" which can be established experientially in the here and now, while others suggest that such realities must wait until the afterlife to receive confirmation. In either case the claim is that this experiential dimension of God-talk renders it cognitively meaningful. While this perspective has a good deal to be said for it, it must be acknowledged that establishing and/or confirming such religious facts is a very difficult task at best, and one that is a long way from completion.

Along with the foregoing responses, there have always been thinkers, both religious and nonreligious, who contend that the verifiability criterion is much too narrow, even for science itself, let alone for philosophy. Many specific criticisms have been raised about the "meaningfulness" (!) of some of the terms used to state and explain the verifiability criterion itself, and serious question has been raised about the status of the criterion according to its own specifications. To put it bluntly, does the criterion itself conform to its own requirements? Perhaps it is really a definition or a proposal for science only. This sort of question opened up many related and increasingly more important issues concerning the various dimensions of meaningfulness within the various regions of language. Ayer and others have sought to modify their perspective as a result of this sort of critique, but in essence they have not altered its main thrust. Nonetheless, fewer and fewer philosophers and theologians now take the early analytic posture very seriously.

Undoubtedly the strongest force contributing to the broader development of linguistic philosophy was the later work of Wittgenstein.[4] After finishing his first book, the *Tractatus*, he "retired" from philosophy (at the age of twenty-five!) because he felt that if he was correct, philosophy was now essentially complete. Some fifteen years later he returned to Cambridge University and devoted the rest of his life to pursuing an approach to philosophy that was fundamentally opposed to his early work. The pivotal point of his fresh posture, expressed most thoroughly in his book, *Philosophical Investigations*, was that language is an extremely complex and diverse phenomenon that cannot be reduced to a single explanation or criterion of meaning. Moreover, he continually stressed that language is essentially a social activity inextricably interwoven with other aspects of human life. It is more like the various games and shared activities we enter into than it is like logic and mathematics.

The ramifications of the later Wittgenstein's approach for those who would use language religiously are considerable. Without claiming that this approach solves all the relevant problems, I suggest that the exploration of God-talk grounded in the insights of more recent linguistic philosophy (often termed "ordinary language analysis") is far more fruitful than any of the postures discussed above. They all have valuable points to make, but until the very board on which the whole game is played is restructured, no real progress can be made. Philosophers such as J. L. Austin, John Wisdom, and Max Black, and theologians such as Ian Ramsey, Basil Mitchell, and David Burrell who have followed the later Wittgenstein's lead seem to me to make the most headway.[5]

One of the more helpful analyses of God-talk from a Wittgensteinian perspective was offered by Ian Ramsey.[6] He called attention to the twofold thrust of most theological and biblical language. On the one hand, such talk is nearly always grounded in human experience by the use of terms like "father," "king," "wise," "loving," and so on. On the other hand, these terms are generally joined with terms that indicate that the initial ones are not to be taken literally but analogically, such as "heavenly," "eternal," "all," or "infinitely." Thus we speak of God as "heavenly Father," "all wise," and "infinitely loving." Ramsey called the former terms "models," because they refer to aspects of experience with which we are very familiar and which encapsulate characteristics we value highly. He called the latter terms "qualifiers," because they instruct us as to how to use the model terms.

In Ramsey's view, and in mine, the terms "heavenly" and "infinite" are not to be taken literally, as referring to physical space and time, but metaphorically, so as to point out talk of God in two directions at once, toward the tangible dimension of experience *and* toward the intangible, more comprehensive dimension which it mediates. The qualifying aspect of our talk of God does not call attention to a different, higher "realm," but rather to a deeper, richer dimension within and throughout our everyday life. Far from divesting religious language of its meaning and force, this interpretation enlivens and expands it by making it both experiential, which was the valid concern of those proposing the verifiability criterion, and yet "more," which is the legitimate theological issue.

To speak of God-talk as essentially metaphorical in nature opens up a whole, and as yet rather unexplored, territory.[7] Although this is not the place to launch into a detailed account of the issues and alternatives involved, perhaps a brief further word would be helpful. By its very nature, metaphorical speech is two-dimensional. That is, it signifies one aspect of reality by means of another. Analogy, paradox, and irony all participate in this general function of language, so it is not surprising that they, too, should be employed in religious speech. For in talking of God we are talking of a transcendent reality by using the only language that we have, namely that through which we speak of and interact with our everyday world. Metaphor enables us to speak of this transcendent reality, while at the same time speaking of our common, everyday life. This view of the meaning of religious language carries with it the possibility of speech which is at once cognitively meaningful and capable of signifying the divine.

EXISTENCE AND MEANING

The other main branch of contemporary philosophy that has had such a powerful impact on the humanities is existentialism.[8] Whereas linguistic philosophy stresses linguistic meaningfulness, existential philosophy emphasizes the meaningfulness of human existence. Although more difficult than any other movement to generalize about, existentialism can be usefully discussed in terms of its positive and negative thrusts. There is also a major distinction within the movement between religious and nonreligious existentialists. We shall first consider the negative thrust, since in many ways this perspective arose as a protest against both traditional and analytic philosophy. Religious existentialists figure more especially into the positive thrust, and hence they will be taken up further on in our discussion.

To begin with, existentialist thinkers may be said to be in protest *against modern civilization* to the degree that it dehumanizes our existence, substituting for inherent human values certain extraneous notions such as "progress," "convenience," "objectivity," and "success." It is claimed that contemporary existence teaches us to treat human beings as mere objects; as vast collections of statistics to be manipulated; as economic markets, political pawns, and low-cost labor. In this technological age, computers especially have become the symbols of the highest level of understanding, and people are urged to emulate them. We are all seen as victims of totalitarian oppression, whether militarily, politically, psychologically, or economically. We live in an age when individualism is systematically stamped out.

Second, existentialist thinkers stand in protest *against rationalism* in both its systematic and analytic modes. In their view, far too much emphasis and confidence have been placed on the role and value of reason in human existence. The entire history of philosophy, with a few exceptions such a Socrates, Pascal, and Nietzsche, sought to systemize and speculate about the "essence" of reality and human nature. Existentialist thinkers are united in their insistence that "existence is prior to essence," that we must choose *how* we live before we have all the data about *what* life is. As Kierkegaard put it: "Life is only understood backwards; it is *lived* forwards." Reason's role, according to existentialists, has been vastly overrated. What good are fancy philosophical systems if the humans who create and extoll them do not have their own lives in order?

Third, exististentialism may be understood as a protest

against traditional religion. Hand in hand with traditional philosophy has gone institutionalized religion, with all of its narrow and esoteric doctrines, as well as its stultifying and empty rituals. Worst of all are its outdated and conventional moral codes, which enslave the majority while allowing a few to live by a double standard. Traditional religion is viewed as being more interested in preserving itself than in being helpful to humankind, as claiming to have all the answers without even really knowing the questions. Moreover, in the twentieth century, after two world wars and the invention of "the bomb," the concept of God as the One who controls human history is at best irrelevant and at worst downright tragic. As both Nietzsche and Dostoevsky said, and as reiterated by Sartre in our century, "God is dead. Anything is possible." The nonreligious existentialists, at least, take this as their point of departure, both theoretically and morally speaking.

Apart from Kierkegaard, who is best classified as a religious existentialist, no thinker has done a more thorough job of cataloging the absurdities and negativities of human life than Martin Heidegger in his book *Being and Time.* In this work Heidegger analyzes the "thrownness" of existence in relation to our origins—we just turn up, without any say in the matter. He also itemizes the various feelings which dominate our emotional life, the fears and anxieties. Finally, he depicts human existence as confronted with the final nothingness of being by the anticipation of death. Amidst all these negativities we are urged to aim at "authenticity," at a way of life that stands on its own and is open to whatever comes.

This brings us to the positive thrust of the existentialist movement. Sartre has argued that "existentialism is a humanism,"[9] that it is an optimistic point of view because it is both realistic about the human situation and enthusiastic about our opportunities. Having been freed from the structure and comfort of traditional philosophy and religion, we are in a position to take full *responsibility* for our own decisions and values. We no longer can or need to hide behind such concepts as God and human nature, to blame fate or our parents or who we are and who we shall yet become. Standing on our own, we are free to create, to invent, to choose our destiny, even though it must be done within the limits of absurdity and the unknown. We are at last free to *be* authentic, to "accept the benign indifference of the universe" (borrowing from Albert Camus's *The Stranger*.

Existentialist thinkers, secondly, having placed such a strong emphasis on the role of choice in human existence, generally go on to urge full *involvement* in those activities which will better the human situation. To work to relieve the suffering of others, to counteract evil wherever it is encountered, is the chief obligation of authentic human existence. This obligation is not based in the law of God, or in some abstract concept of "duty," but simply in the fact that we are all human beings, abandoned in an absurd world—and, after all, pain hurts. We should not be under any illusions that our efforts to alleviate suffering and counter injustice will contribute to the final victory of "the Good," to any sort of utopian kingdom on earth. We are like Sisyphus, doomed for eternity to roll our huge rock up the hill, only to watch it roll to the bottom again. Nevertheless, the existentialists urge, we can stand tall in the knowledge that life has no meaning other than that which we give it—and we can *choose* to give it meaning by the integrity with which we live it.

At this point religious extistentialists take one further step. Nonreligious existentialists view this extra step as irresponsible and self-deceiving, but thinkers like Kierkegaard, Gabriel Marcel, Jaques Maritain, and Paul Tillich contend that after acknowledging the stark realities of our existence and the necessity of our free responsibility, we must also, through *faith*, commit ourselves to God, the source and meaning of our existence. To live as if we were in fact fully responsible for our own existence and destiny is said to be both arrogant and the height of irresponsibility. We must acknowledge that amidst the absurdities and narrow limitations of life we are creatures who find their authenticity and completeness only in relationship to the One who created us.

Kierkegaard's analysis of the three spheres of existence provides an excellent perspective on religious existentialism.[10] He suggested that each of us, at various times and in various degrees, participate in one or more of the following levels or modes of existence. It is our responsibility to discern and choose our own existential "location." To begin with, there is the *aesthetic mode*, wherein a person remains unaware that he or she *is* a self, or could *become* a self. Such persons are continuously on the go, burying themselves in "the immediate," systematically avoiding the responsibility of and the opportunity to choose selfhood. These aesthetes may lose themselves in a wide variety of activities, many of which may well be worthwhile in and of themselves. The point is not *what* is done, but *how* and *why* it is done.

Next, there is the *ethical mode*. The person living at this level has chosen to face the responsibility of selfhood, to rise above the immediate and make a commitment that involves the future and other persons. Kierkegaard would commend nonreligious existentialists, such as Camus and Sartre, for embodying this mode of existence. They have faced the world and themselves, taking responsibility for who and what they become. The difficulty is, according to Kierkegaard, that such persons choose to be selves *by themselves*, apart from any relationship to God. They stop short of the religious mode, the highest sphere of human existence.

The *religious mode* of existence has two phases or "movements." The first is represented by "The Knight of Infinite Resignation," the person who chooses to be a self but realizes that he or she cannot in any way acheive this alone. The second movement is lived out by "The Knight of Faith," the person who chooses to be a self, not alone, but in relation to God. Kierkegaard illustrates this Knight of Faith with Abraham, in his powerful work, *Fear and Trembling*. He describes Abraham's double movement, when called by God to sacrifice his only son Isaac. Abraham faced the absurd (God had originally promised to give him a large family and nation through Isaac) with authenticity—he accepted his responsibility, resigned himself to the inevitable, and yet believed that God would provide.

Taking stock of existentialism, there is, to my mind, a great deal for people of faith to learn from this movement. Many of its criticisms of contemporary civilization, for instance, are right on target. Even though such practices were not invented in the modern age, our culture does emphasize externalities and often treats human beings as if they were mere objects. In addition, the existentialist's suspicions about the limitations of rationalism are fairly well grounded. Historically, this tradition has been overly dualistic and "otherwordly" in its emphasis. Even its empiricist competitors have defined reason much too narrowly and sought to impose it much too broadly. Reason as it generally is conceived by philosophers, while extremely valuable, fails to consider other important aspects of human life.

The existentialist critique of traditional religion and theology is also worth a great deal of consideration. Far too often the church has "played God" in the affairs of the world and individuals alike. In general, wherever Christianity has become the "official" religion, there has been a tendency to equate God and country, to identify being a Christian with certain external "upright" behavior, and to expect everyone to conform to these standards. As Kierkegaard said, "When everyone is a Christian, no one is a Christian." Moreover, theology has far too frequently been an abstract, irrelevant enterprise that reflects the cultural and moral bias of those engaged in it, and it has often failed to address the real issues of its day. It is extremely important for faith to be integrated with all of life, and for individual believers to be *personally* committed to God, not just culturally and/or intellectually.

At the same time, however, I have certain reservations about existentialism. As long as it is understood as a protest against certain imbalances in Western thought and culture, existentialism makes a vital contribution. When it is offered or taken as a basis for a sound and comprehensive approach to human life, however, then it appears to be an imbalance itself. Human existence is at bottom every bit as social and historical as it is individual and existential. We live in relationship and community, out of the past and toward the future, as well as on our own in the here and now. A helpful view of life and faith takes this into account more than existentialist thinkers generally do.

Philosophically, the existentialist posture strikes me as legitimate in its protest against the narrowness of traditional philosophy's view of reason, but as wide of the mark in its seemingly irrational reaction to this narrowness. Rather than hand over the criteria and procedures of reason to the standard "objectivist" approaches, it would seem more helpful to call for a fresh, broader interpretation of cognitivity in general. This is especially important with respect to the relation between reason and faith, if we are to be able to keep them distinct from each other without separating them. I shall make some proposals along this line in the by now over-advertised chapter 7.

Theologically, it seems important to develop a deeper and more generally applicable notion of faith than existentialist thinkers offer. While it must not be a slave to reason and/or tradition, faith must also be thoroughly integrated with every aspect of our lives, and in the broad sense it must be "reasonable" or responsible. It is not enough to believe something to be true, to fervently commit oneself to a cause, an idea, or a person, irrespective of cognitive factors. Such a conception of faith justifies too much, for it opens the door to any and every cause that comes down the pike. A faith that is honoring to God must at least be concerned about whether and/or which God is real, as well as about the most authentic way to worship and serve God.

Suggested Reading

Carnell, E. J. *Christian Commitment.* New York: Macmillan, 1982.

Hick, John. *Philosophy of Religion.* Englewood Cliffs, NJ: Prentice-Hall, 1983.

Richardson, Herbert. *Transcendence.* Boston: Beacon, 1969.

Tillich, Paul. *The Dynamics of Faith.* New York: Harper & Row, 1975.

The Arts: 5
Subjectivism

GENERALLY SPEAKING, the arts are not considered to be particularly relevant to the dialogue between the academy and Christian faith. In fact, it is not too far off the mark to suggest that the arts have been essentially ignored by many Christians, especially those of a more conservative posture. Throughout the Christian era the church has either condemned image-making altogether or totally confined it within the scope of its own purposes. In modern times, however, since the arts have "come of age," the two have pretty much gone their separate ways. My concern in this chapter is to enliven the interaction between faith and the arts by directly addressing both the traditional relationship between them and their current estrangement.

REPRESENTATION AND EXPRESSION

Until very recent times it was generally assumed that the purpose of art was to *represent* some specific, external aspect of the world, whether human, natural, or divine. Statues, portraits, landscapes, and "program music" (such as "Peter and the Wolf" and "The Overture of 1812") were the order of the day. The basic idea was to create an imitation or representation which resembled the subject matter as closely as possible. As early as Plato this notion of art as imitation was the accepted view, and it was because of the possible abuses of the art's representational capacity that Plato was highly cautious about their place in the ideal society.

There was, of course, an emotional correlate to this view in relation to what the work of art was supposed to do in the viewer or listener. This idea was forcefully expressed by Aristotle in terms of the idea of "catharsis," a notion which dominated aesthetic theory for more than two thousand years. His point was simply that an effective work of art is one that touches a corresponding chord in the viewer or listener and triggers a release or cleansing of emotional energy.

This representational perspective was pretty well taken over by the church down through the ages in religious art. Those who did not forbid the use of art in worship, on the grounds that image-making is always idolatrous, employed the arts as a means of representing spiritual realities and inspiring specific spiritual virtues in the worshiper. Thus even today the vast majority of people, perhaps especially Christians, assume that art is "religious" when it is about religious persons, events, or themes, and that it is "secular" when it is not. In short, subject matter is generally considered to be the central concern of art, with the degree of realism constituting the criterion of aesthetic value.

It is because of the preponderance of this perspective that one so frequently hears, when visiting museums and galleries, remarks like "What's *that* supposed to be?" and "It doesn't look much like a woman (or house, bridge, etc.) to me." In like manner, Christians generally value works of art more if they are "about" religious topics or if they find them "moving" religiously, irrespective of their relative aesthetic merits. Conversely, works of art are often judged as inferior or immoral because they represent nonreligious or sexual themes or topics. Why I take this view to be fundamentally mistaken and unfruitful religiously will become clear as this chapter progresses.

With the advent of Impressionism, the focus of art began to shift from the external world toward the personal world of the artist.[1] This shift of emphasis gave rise to what we now call "modern art." The Impressionists sought more to portray the external world as they experienced it or as it appeared to them, rather than as it is in and of itself. They focused on the relational reality comprised of the perceiver's *interaction* with the world rather than on an exact representation of it. This shift in perspective was given additional impetus by the invention of photography. Many people reasoned that since the camera provides a far better copy of the world than the artist can, art must either have a different purpose or go out of business altogether.

The next development was what is known as "abstract Expressionism." Many artists came to feel that it is more important for a work of art to express the feelings of its creator than to represent anything in the objective world. The emphasis now shifted to the internal, subjective world of the artist. Roughly simultaneous with this modern shift of focus from the outside to the inside came a decreasing interest in religious themes. In the last hundred years or so, artists have no longer been restricted to work under the patronage of either the church or the aristocracy. Modern art has been pretty much "art for art's sake." Artists want to "make a statement" of their own.

The results of this overall revolution have been confusing, to say the least. Traditionalists, including many religious folk, have never ceased to lament this development as the clear-cut abdication of artistic responsibility to society, to beauty, and to God. The modern artist is often viewed as self-centered and decadent, as symbolic of the increasing materialism and secularism of our civilization. On the other hand, many see modern art as the first stage in the actual birth of "true art." They think that art, like science, can only be itself and make its greatest contribution to society when it is free from religious and political restraints. Some even go so far as to claim that "pure art" is the last and only mode of expression of the ultimate values of individuality and creativity.

What does all this have to do with Christian faith? In many ways the foregoing developments and debates parallel those in theology. Traditionally theology has been concerned with a *realistic* account of divine reality and has defined faith as belief in these objective truths. In modern times many have come to think of theology as the symbolic expression of spiritual truths and of faith as subjective and ethical commitment to them. Here, too, the shift has been from the external to the internal, from Representationism to Expressionism. Many believers feel as confused by the revolution in art as they are by that in theology, though they are less knowledgeable and less concerned about art. Is there any way to overcome the extremes and dichotomies in these areas, any way to combine the values of both sides while avoiding the liabilities?

Postponing the theological/philosophical aspect of these issues until chapter 7, let me offer a suggestion as to how we can better understand the arts in and of themselves, and in their relationship to faith. I think what is most helpful is to think of art as aiming not at the representation of the world or at the expression of the artist, but at the *participation* of the viewer or listener. As I see it, art has always been seeking to *engage* the "prehender," the person who encounters it, not just at the emotional level but at every level of human experience. Clearly, the feelings and insights of the artist are involved in this process, as are those features which comprise the external world, even if only as colors, shapes, and sounds arranged in nonrepresentational patterns. But these factors, necessary as they are, are only the means by which the *interaction* of the prehender is sought. Art is, after all, a form of symbolic communication, a way of sharing between persons around a common task or theme.

The traditional way of thinking of art, as mere representation of objective reality, relies too exclusively on the imitation theory to do justice to the obvious creative dimension of artistic activity. The modern interpretation of art, as primarily an expression of the artist's feelings or insights, is too individualistic to do justice to the clear-cut material and social dimensions of the artistic process. Thinking of art as a means of symbolic communication, in and through the features of the world and the feelings of the artist, enables us to avoid

the passivity of the traditional view and the individualism of
the modern view. In this way, aesthetic reality and value are
understood as *relational* in character, rather than as objective
or as subjective, seeking the involvement of the prehender.

This approach to understanding artistic activity shifts our
focus from asking, "What is the artist saying about the world
or him or herself?" to asking, "How does the work speak to
us, what does it tell us about ourselves?" This is not to suggest that art is subjective, that "Beauty is in the eye of the
beholder" only, but rather that the primary purpose of art is
to evoke a response, to engage the prehender in a dialogue
with the artist and other prehenders about the features of a
given work, together with the themes and feelings which they
mediate. Thus, rather than the main question's being, "What
does this work (or artist) mean, how shall we interpret it?" we
should rather ask, "What are the possibilities here and what
do they tell me about myself?" It may well be necessary to
explore the realistic (or at least the material) features of the
work, as well as various aspects of the artist's life and ideas,
but these should not be the primary considerations.

The implications of this approach to art for faith are considerable. Instead of *expecting* works of art or artists to depict
religious themes or to teach spiritual "messages" as such, we
ought rather to examine the particulars of the work with an
eye to discerning what the work or the artist is saying to and
about us as fellow human beings. Similarly, we ought not
begin by *evaluating* the work, or the artist, from within our
own preconceived perspective, but allow the aesthetic aspects
to probe and perhaps challenge our own values and commitments. What initially appears to be irrelevant or contrary to
religious belief may turn out to be just the opposite. And, by
the same token, just because a painting, song, or poem is
about Christian themes does not mean that it is of aesthetic
value—or even that, at the deepest level, it really embodies
spiritual truth.

By way of illustration and substantiation of this interpretation of the relation between faith and art, consider Jesus' use

of parable as his primary mode of teaching.[2] The parable is
an aesthetic device, a work of art, which while not representing actual people and events (let alone religious ones) seeks
to engage the hearer and evoke a response in relation to certain spiritual realities. The point was not and is not to evaluate the parables of Jesus, either with regard to their creative
"technique" or in terms of their "realism," but rather to interact with them in the sense of allowing them to interpret
and evaluate us at the deepest level. My suggestion is that
works of art, whether ancient or modern, whether ostensibly
religious or not, may well serve the same general purpose in
the life of the Christian.

FORMALISM AND POLITICISM

The foregoing debate between Representationism and Expressionism embodies but one facet of the multifaceted discussion about the nature of art and its relation to religious
belief. Another important facet of this discussion is that of
the debate between Formalism and Politicism. There are
those who maintain that the true nature of art, the highest
criterion of aesthetic value, consists in the particular configuration of formal or abstract qualities inherent in a given
work. This approach is termed *Formalism* and is at least as old
as Plato. In its metaphysical interpretation, Formalism
stresses the primacy of abstract conception and definition.
The idea is that since material reality is logically and ontolog-
ically dependent on formal or conceptual reality, true and
great art must be that which most nearly mirrors the perfect
and unchanging abstract relationship among qualities. The
extreme of this point of view is taken by those thinkers who
actually argue (e.g. Croce) that a great work of art need only,
perhaps *ought* only, exist in the mind of the artist, without
ever being "contaminated" through representation in the material world.

The more concrete interpretation of Formalism would concentrate on the formal characteristics of a work of art as they

are *embodied* in the actual features of that work, in the lines, shapes, colors, sounds, rhythms, and the like. The stress is not upon subject matter, or on the feelings of either the artist or the prehender, but is rather on the particular formal patterns and qualities exhibited by the work in question. It is said that it is the artist's use of such features that constitutes the work's aesthetic value, the specific employment of the medium involved that comprises its unique reality. This interpretation would suggest that it is only by focusing on the formal qualities of works of art that we can ascertain their true worth, since it is only these features that can be universally valuable across different times and cultures. Any other focus, on content, style, or feelings, for example, will fall victim of relativism and not yield absolute aesthetic value.

At the opposite end of the continuum stand those who maintain that art is primarily a social phenomenon, one whose essential purpose is to communicate ideas, moving people emotionally and behaviorally. For lack of a better term we might call this approach *Politicism* because it stresses the cultural and practical dimensions of artistic activity. One version of this posture is expressed by those who emphasize art as a function of social and domestic interaction, as in "preliterate" societies and "folk art." This more anthropological interpretation looks with suspicion on those who would abstract art from its social and practical matrix, making it into a specialty of those with advanced educational and economic standing. It was precisely this type of thinking that led Europeans to conclude that African people had no art because they had no museums. The true nature of art is more aptly revealed, according to this form of Politicism, by the statement made by a person in Bali, "We have no 'art'; we simply try to make everything as well as we can."

Another version of this general posture is that espoused by certain Communist thinkers who claim that all aspects of culture ought to serve the concrete needs of the working class, either to raise their consciousness in countries where they are oppressed or to inspire them to higher levels of cooperative productivity in postrevolutionary countries.[3] This interpretation is disdainful of all Western nations of art because they have been developed within the structures and purposes of the ruling class and as such are elitist, individualistic, and decadent. These thinkers are quick to point out that in spite of all the talk about aesthetic value, whether among Representationalists, Expressionists, or Formalists, art has always been and remains a function of concrete economic factors controlled by those in power. In capitalistic countries this is especially evident, for it is art collectors, museum directors, and gallery owners who largely determine which works and which artists are "valuable." The person who pays the fiddler, after all, is the one who chooses the tune.

A third form of this general "political" approach to art may be found within the church. Down through the ages, art has served the needs and purposes of religion, whether in preliterate, Eastern, or Western cultures. The Medieval church, as well as modern Roman Catholicism, used and essentially controlled various art forms in many periods and places. Early Protestantism, reacting against what were perceived as idolatrous abuses of image-making, took a dim view of the use of art in the church, but in time this gave way to a healthier integration of the two in most denominations. Nevertheless, there has been a strong tendency, especially among conservative Christians, to employ and evaluate artistic expression on the basis of its conformity to certain preconceived, nonaesthetic purposes. Certain rhythms and subject matter, as well as certain language and implied morals, have been deemed unsuitable and thus of less worth by various church groups.

It seems to me that it is possible to find a "middle way" among all these different emphases, one that integrates their insights and avoids their shortcomings. To begin with, I think Formalism has an extremely valuable point to make. Speaking *purely aesthetically*, it would seem that it is the qualitative characteristics, rather than content, feelings, and use of a work of art that should determine its artistic value. What a work is "about," what it tells us of the artist's feelings and insights, whatever emotions it inspires, and however it may be employed culturally, all of these things are interesting in their own right and important for other reasons (historically, psychologically, anthropologically, and so on). But they are not the central issue from an aesthetic perspective. It is the configuration of the specific elements inherent in the particular medium that renders a product a work of art and upon which its aesthetic worth should be based.

At the same time, however, because art is, after all, a human activity involving skill and effort, and because only embodied skill and effort can be experienced and evaluated, it seems essential to stress the necessity of the concrete expression of the formal elements of art in actual physical media. Moreover, it is the incarnation of these elements that makes artistic activity available and valuable to other persons, both individually and culturally. It is my conviction that art is a form of symbolic communication. Clearly, such a view necessitates concrete, perceptual qualities to serve as the bearers of meaning.

This way of thinking brings us to the heart of the matter with respect to art. In the previous section I suggested overcoming the dichotomy between representation and expression by focusing on participation. In this context I would recommend mediating between Formalism and Politicism by directing attention to the fact that art is, after all, an activity or *process*. In short, I would submit that the most helpful way to think about art is in terms of the *interaction* between the artist and the medium on the one hand and between the completed work and the prehender(s) on the other. The artist is engaged in a dialogue with his or her medium, shaping it to fit the vision and altering the vision to fit the requirements of the medium. In like manner, the prehender is engaged in a dialogue with the completed work, addressing and exploring it as well as being addressed and explored by it.[4]

The value of the politicist interpretation of art arises when the above characterization is applied at the social level. For, as we have seen, art is a form of symbolic communication that takes place in a "multifaceted," "thick" weave of human interaction in actual historical, political, and economic circumstances. Thus, while engaged in their respective dialogues with the work of art, both the artist and the prehender are at the same time interacting with concrete cultural traditions and patterns, simultaneously altering and being altered by them. Focusing on the participatory and process orientation of aesthetic activity and awareness provides a way to integrate the formal and political aspects of art.

The significance of all this for religious belief may be summarized in the following way. While stressing the formalistic aspects of art may seem to render it irrelevant to religion, as emphasizing the political aspects may seem to place art under the control of religion, focusing on the process of aesthetic activity and awareness casts light on some important parallels between the two. To begin with, there is the parallel between the artist's creative efforts and abilities and those of God. The Judeo-Christian Scriptures frequently liken God's creative activity to those of a potter and a builder-architect. Moreover, it is fruitful to think of God's ongoing involvement with the world, striving to bring the creation to its ultimate redemptive fulfillment, as similar to that of an artist interacting with his or her medium. In neither case is the creative process a static, unilateral, assembly-line enterprise. The struggles and adjustments are real, as a visit to any artist's studio or a careful reading of the Judeo-Christian Scriptures will make clear.

Most significant, however, is the importance of this particular way of understanding aesthetic awareness for our view of the nature of revelation and faith. Far too frequently Christians limit their concept of revelation to propositions which reveal information about spiritual matters that would otherwise be unknown, and their notion of faith is the act of giving intellectual assent to these propositions. Such an approach corresponds to viewing art strictly in terms of subject matter, formal quality, and/or sociopolitical edification. A process and participatory approach to these notions emphasizes that revelation, in the Judeo-Christian understanding, takes place in concrete historical and community events, while faith is understood as the believer's interaction with and commitment to what is revealed thereby from within this tradition and community.

The most obvious substantiation of this view of revelation is found in the very notion of Incarnation itself. The Word did not remain an abstract concept, but rather became flesh, entering into the human form of life as the embodiment of God's love and grace. God is the artist, and the divine message, or "statement," is encountered in the person of Christ in interaction with his tradition and contemporaries. In like fashion, faith in the Scriptures is never defined as mental assent to mere doctrines, but as the total commitment of the whole person to the spiritual reality mediated in and through the Incarnation. Such participatory interaction is essentially parallel to that of the prehender engaged by the artist's creative activity embodied in and mediated through the concrete medium of his or her choice.

Absurdism and Censorship

In recent decades, contemporary art has developed in a wide variety of directions and modes. Most of these recent developments have been greeted initially with shock and rejection, only to find eventual acceptance through increased familiarity. By and large the religious community has remained at best skeptical of, if not downright horrified by, nearly all contemporary art. Perhaps the primary reason for the difficult reception of new styles and techniques has been the fact that the vast majority of works in nearly every field have been *experimental* in character. Artists today simply do not want to repeat what has already been done by someone else. Moreover, they are excited about challenging the traditional assumptions concerning what constitutes art and how it is to be made and appreciated. Indeed, there is great value in experimentation and revolution in every field, from science through business to religion. There are also risks and potential abuses inherent in these processes which need to be acknowledged.[5]

In painting, the revolution began with the cubist movement, which experimented with perspective and geometric planes. Picasso was a forerunner here. Surrealism followed this lead by giving a dreamlike quality to everyday objects, as in the works of Salvadore Dali. Jackson Pollack developed the idea of throwing, pouring, and squirting paint around on a large canvas which was lying on the floor, while Modrian and Kandinsky worked with a few lines and shapes arranged in simple geometric patterns. Then some painters sought ever more simple works, such as black on white or white on white, while others, such as Jasper Johns, actually built objects like shoes, cans, and coat-hangers into their paintings in unpredictable arrangements. Still others have developed extremely "realistic" techniques, painting everyday scenes of contemporary life that are actually mistaken for photographs.

In sculpture, similar developments occurred. Artists such as Henry Moore were influenced by African and Eskimo styles, emphasizing the geometric form and "negative space" in their human figures. Some sculptors, like Brancusi, developed a cubist style, while others shifted to other media, such as plastic, fiberglass, and epoxy. Welding uncommon objects and pieces of metal into abstract geometric forms has become an important dimension of sculpture.

Both music and drama, as well as dance, have followed along in this experimental and revolutionary mode. Schoenburg and John Cage led the way in forcing the West to rethink the relationship between sound and music by employing heretofore unused tones (and even the noise of traffic) in musical compositions. Beckett and others pioneered in the "theater of the absurd," forcing the audience to forge its own connections and meanings in plays without traditional plots. Pirandello and Grotowski went further, calling into question the very notions of "audience," "dialogue," and "actors." Traditional ballet has had to share the dance stage with more free-form styles such as Modern Jazz, Contemporary, and Afro-Caribbean. Even photography has grown from simply reproducing copies of places, people, and things to experimentation with light, texture, perspective, and developing techniques.

Paralleling these various movements and phases in contemporary art has been the development of a whole school of what might best be termed "art educators," rather than artists *per se*, who have challenged the very notion of art itself. Marcel Duchamps led the way here by actually exhibiting a urinal in an art museum. His idea was that art is whatever anyone wants it to be, that we ought to open our eyes to the aesthetic realities in the everyday objects which surround us. This opened the way to "found art," in which artists displayed common objects in an artistic way. Eventually this led to "conceptual art," wherein artists turned everyday activities, such as picking up one's mail or hanging out the wash, into museum pieces by actually doing these things in museums. More recently several artists have made news by stretching various kinds of materials across large open spaces or around a group of islands. The point here, again, is "art is where you find (or put) it."

Now, what is to be made of all this, and what, if anything, does it have to say to Christian belief? There are, to be sure, those who would say that it is all hopelessly absurd, worthless, and totally subjective—and that as such it is either devoid of any religious value or is indeed diabolical. While I am prepared to acknowledge that a good deal of what passes for art today is at best misnamed, I do think it is important not to be too hasty in passing judgment, lest we fail to learn and profit from what is valuable in all of this ferment. A solid, biblical faith is always open to fresh developments, for God is always doing "a new thing"; the number one sin of the "chosen people," in both the Old and New Testaments was their infernal tendency to confuse their own understandings and practices with eternal truth.

To be more specific, the antics of some of the Old Testament "heroes" would appear, if we were not so familiar with them, every bit as bizarre and absurd as those of contemporary artists. The signs performed by Moses and Aaron, most of which were duplicated by Pharaoh's magicians, were quite irregular. And the behavior of many of the prophets was anything but conventional. Amos wore a signboard advertising Israel's sin, Hosea married a harlot and named his children things like "not pitied," while Jeremiah bought worthless land to dramatize his belief that Israel would return from captivity. Surely Daniel and Ezekiel's behavior was as shocking to their contemporaries as the work of many artists is to us.

To be even more specific, Jesus himself was continually challenging the accepted way of doing and saying things. His primary conflict was with the most orthodox and religious folk of his day. He repeatedly reinterpreted the Scriptures in ways that openly contradicted established teachings. He often did unacceptable things like spitting in public and doing good on the Sabbath, and he was condemned for hanging around with unsavory people. After the fact, it is all too easy for us to say about the prophets as well as Jesus, "Yes, but they were acting on behalf of God." The fact is, however, the most orthodox people of their day did not see the activity of God in their outlandish behavior; it was only with the test of time that such values are discerned.

The point I am making here is simply that we should not be too quick to judge whatever does not conform to our traditional standards of value, whether religiously or aesthetically. I am not suggesting that we condone every artistic innovation that comes along, but it certainly behooves us to remain open to the possibility that new wine may demand new wineskins. To begin with, it is imperative to be able to give an empathetic ear and/or eye to fresh developments, to explore and seek to appreciate where they are coming from and what they are up to. This applies with special force to religious uses of art, for fresh modes of expression are needed here as well as in art in general. Simply to reject innovations because they seem absurd is a shallow form of "moralism" that has no place in a strong Christian faith posture.

There are those who would condemn the whole of modern and/or contemporary art as being a denial of the transcendent dimension of existence. They would argue that all forms of modernity are essentially humanistic and/or naturalistic, and as such are in conflict with a theistic understanding of reality. One conservative Christian author maintains that this conflict is symbolized in Rubens' painting of Plato and Aristotle by the fact that, as they walk along, the former is pointing up while the latter is pointing down. He also argues that Michelangelo's unfinished statues represent a naturalistic, evolutionary view of human nature. There are, as well, more sophisticated forms of this point of view within the Christian community.

Aside from the obvious point that these particular works of art are clearly subject to alternative interpretations, the chief difficulty with this general approach is that it is based on a naïve and outmoded understanding of art as essentially representational. Generally, according to this view, art is *about* something, seeks to tell us how reality is; thus when it is "about" some religious theme or topic it is valuable religiously, and when it is not it is not. My own suggestion is that a better criterion by which to evaluate art in general and religious art in particular is an *incarnational* one. That is, to focus on the work or elements of the medium in such a way as to discern what reality is being mediated thereby and what this signifies for our own values and mode of existence. It should be apparent that in using such a criterion many paintings and songs, for instance, which are generally thought to be religious will turn out not to be, while many that make no claim to be religious will prove to be so. This is not unlike what Jesus said in Matthew 25 about the two different kinds of people who will be judged according to what they *did*, not what they *said*.

Another way to put all this is to suggest that the best criterion for ascertaining the religious value of a given work or mode of art is not what is its subject matter, or who is the artist, but whether or not it has aesthetic quality and integrity. Although one must make allowances for individual taste and stages of growth, whenever such things are roughly equal, a truly fine though "secular" poem, play, song, or painting will be of more value religiously than a "religious" work that is poorly done. In my opinion, then, Beethoven's music, Rembrandt's paintings, and Shakespeare's plays are more valuable both aesthetically and *religiously* (the latter because of the former) than such "Christian" works as the song "In the Garden," Salman's painting of the "Head of Christ," and Cardinal Spellman's novel, *The Foundling.*

All of which brings us directly to the issue of Christian censorship. Just what should be the Christian's policy toward exposure to works of art that not only do not portray life directly from a Christian point of view, but which in content or tone seem to be contrary to that point of view? This issue has two levels, the public and private. With respect to public policy, it seems to me that while Christians have every right and a certain responsibility to "leaven" the community mix with Christian values, we must remember that in principle (constitutionally) as well as in practice (sociologically) we live in a secular (neither holy nor profane), pluralistic society. Thus the rights of those who differ from us, even if they are in the minority, must be respected in a way that they were not in Calvin's Geneva or in Puritan Boston. Freedom *of* religion also means the possibility of freedom *from* religion, if one so chooses.

On the private level, it is interesting to reflect on the fact that in Paul's day the person of stronger faith was the one who had no need of moral censorship (e.g., eating meat sacrificed to idols, etc.), while the person of weaker faith was the one who lived more restrictedly. Today things are often the reverse, with the stronger faith supposedly the one who abstains from "the world." I think the New Testament perspective is healthier and more consistent with the incarnational theme of the Word becoming flesh, interacting with and transforming the world rather than judging and withdrawing from it. Jesus was *in* the world, though not *of* it, and Paul says (Col. 1:18) that Christ is to have "preeminence *in* all things," not *instead of* or *above* all things.

Let me conclude with a concrete case in point. A few years ago I had a colleague who taught a film course in a Christian college. In one of our faculty forums she presented her rationale for such a course in such a setting. Several faculty members challenged her with respect to the profanity, sexual immorality, and violence so prevalent in contemporary films. She argued, extremely cogently I thought, that exposure to these films was valuable for three reasons. First, if Christians are going to help people in the world, they must, as Jesus did, go *where* they are and know who they are. Second, Christians have no corner on the wisdom and insight available to humankind, and sometimes at least they can learn from nonbelievers. Third, she suggested that more often than one might suspect, the "non-Christian" film actually does a better job portraying Christian themes than do insipid, clichéd religious films. As a final substantiation and illustration, my colleague gave a detailed analysis of the redemptive qualities of the film, *Midnight Cowboy* (starring Jon Voight and Dustin Hoffman).

My own work with film has centered on those by Ingmar Bergman, and I could have added to my colleague's general point by an examination of Bergman's exploration of the complexities of the human condition, and the need for, and lack of, love and communication. The richness of such works of art, along with many of those mentioned earlier, even with their shortcomings, far outweighs that of most so-called "Christian art." Spiritual reality often reveals itself where we least expect it, even among the least respected "absurdities and subjectivisms."

Suggested Readings

Eversole, Finley. *Christian Faith and the Contemporary Arts.* Nashville: Abingdon, 1962.

Leuchlie, Samuel. *Art and Religion in Conflict.* Philadelphia: Fortress, 1980.

Weismann, Donald. *The Visual Arts As Human Experience.* Englewood Cliffs, NJ: Prentice-Hall, 1974.

Wolterstorff, Nicholas. *Art in Action.* Grand Rapids: Eerdmans, 1980.

World Religions: **6** *Pluralism*

UP TO THIS POINT in our examination of the relationship between Christian faith and the various disciplines comprising the academic enterprise, we have been dealing with issues that arise out of the interface between religion and the sciences, the humanities, and the arts. There is, however, a different sort of challenge that arises from within the study of religion itself, especially as it is frequently studied in departments of religion in colleges and universities. With the continuous shrinking of our world, through increased mobility and communication, we have come now to live in what has been called a "Global Village."

Before this century the peoples and religions of other lands and cultures were thought of as both mysterious and pagan, primarily because we were ignorant of them. Today, however, not only are we exposed to the ways and thoughts of other cultures and religions through the mass media, but we increasingly encounter in our daily lives persons who believe and behave quite differently from us. As we come to broaden our understanding of other peoples we must also rethink our ideas about the nature and value of their religious beliefs. Western Christianity is no longer the only religion on the market, for we now live in a pluralistic multiculture and we must ask, "What is the most helpful way to think about the Christian faith in relation to these other world religions?"

Exclusivism and Inclusivism

The traditional Christian posture toward other religions has been *exclusivistic* in character. That is to say, Christians have generally thought and taught that Christianity is the only true religion; that all the others, no matter how inspiring and/or influential, are either misleading or diabolical. This perspective is sometimes expressed by saying that non-Christian religions are human attempts to reach God, while Christianity is God's act to reach humanity. The focus here is on a strict interpretation of Jesus' words, "I am the Way, the Truth, and the Life; no one comes to the Father except by me." One of the ramifications of such a view is that all those who have not encountered Jesus Christ are beyond God's redemptive activity. Thus the motivation for Christian missionary efforts.

There are, however, several reasons why this traditional posture is increasingly difficult to maintain, at least in its more narrow interpretations. First, there is the difficulty of explaining how the true believers of the Old Testament, who clearly knew nothing of the historical Jesus from Nazareth, are to be counted among the redeemed. This is usually handled by saying that such folk looked *forward* to the Messiah, while we look *back* at him. The fact remains, however, that this "looking forward" in no way involved the sort of understanding of Christ that we generally associate with divine redemption. Indeed, the basis upon which the writers of the New Testament assign redemption to the Old Testament "saints" is their "faith" (see especially Hebrews 11), that is, their capacity to trust God amidst their *contemporary* circumstances.

Second, there is the problem of the vast numbers of people who lived beyond the reach of, indeed on the other side of the world from, both the Hebrew nation and Jesus' brief ministry. Unless one takes an extreme Calvinistic view of election, wherein God's grace is essentially arbitrary, it is very difficult to see how traditional exclusion can be combined with a Christian understanding of God's love and justice. In addition, there are millions of people who have lived and are living since Jesus' time without ever having heard of him. If an encounter with Jesus, in the historical, informational sense, is necessary for their redemption, how can it be their fault that they have not been reached with the message? Perhaps it was to such people that Paul was referring in the second chapter of his letter to the Romans, when he suggests that Gentiles know what is right on the basis of their conscience (part of the image of God from creation), and are justified or not, accordingly.

Third, coming from the opposite direction, I would submit that the whole notion of what constitutes actually *hearing* the Christian message is far more complex than the exclusivist posture acknowledges. Certainly simply being exposed to certain "facts," as pieces of information about Jesus' life and death or Paul's interpretation thereof, is not sufficient. In fact, it is possible that what often passes for "hearing the gospel" in our Western culture is so covered over with commercialism, egotism, exhibitionism, and the like that it is virtually impossible to encounter the Christian message in this way. Thus, it may be that precious few folk have actually had opportunity to hear about Jesus, even within the bounds of Christendom. Similarly, there are many differing interpretations of Jesus' way, truth, and life. Which is the correct one— only our own?

Partly because of such considerations there has developed, in modern times, a perspective on such matters known as *"inclusivism"* or *"syncretism."* According to this view, all religions (at least the major ones) are essentially equal in value, each representing a different way of reaching God; many paths, one goal. Another form of this posture maintains that deep within each of the (major) religions lies a common core that constitutes the real truth about God, the world, and humanity. Sometimes this core is viewed rationalistically, as with the thinkers of the Enlightenment (e.g. John Locke).[1] Or it is thought of in emotional terms, as with the Romanticists (e.g. Friedrich Schleiermacher).[2] There are also those who define this core more in terms of mythic world views and cultural archetypes, as with Mercia Eliade[3] and Carl Jung.[4] Christianity is viewed as one, perhaps the highest, form of this common religious truth that is inclusive of all humankind.

The major difficulty with this type of approach, aside from the fact that it seems impossible to get agreement on what constitutes the common core, is twofold. On the one hand, such total inclusivism completely ignores the fact that there are important differences among world religions, differences which their various adherents are not willing to overlook. At least some world religions are exclusivistic and missionary-minded in character. On the other hand, by "reducing" all religions to one common denominator, inclusivism fails to show real respect for any of them. In fact, the very notion of a common core or universal religion may itself be a product of the Western way of thinking about religion; it may well be incompatible with some non-Western ways of thinking.

Between exclusivism and inclusivism there has arisen an approach known as cultural relativism or *"pluralism."* The basic idea here, as developed by students of the history of religions, is that each religion, like each individual culture, has a value and integrity all its own—otherwise it would never have arisen or survived. This approach seeks to overcome the impasse between the other two views by accepting the reality and viability of each (major) religion (as opposed to exclusivism), while at the same time maintaining the unique irreducibility of each (as opposed to inclusivism). W. Cantwell Smith[5] argues, for instance, that religions, like cultures, are neither true nor false; they either are or are not, they either serve their respective peoples well or they do not. Each must be acknowledged, studied, and evaluated for itself, in relation to its historical and social context.

While I think the above view has a great deal of merit, and

is in many ways to be preferred over the other two approaches, it is not altogether satisfactory. While acknowledging the distinctive and individual character of each religion and culture, it remains possible to speak intelligently and fruitfully about commonalities as well. People, after all, are all people—we have a common form of life that expresses itself in a wide variety of ways. The universality of such features of human life may be accredited without falling into various forms of reductionism. Religion, it would seem, like language and family life of some sort, is a likely candidate for such universality. Almost all peoples have stories and beliefs about their origins, meaning, and destinies that involve "higher" (powerful and wise) beings and other worlds or dimensions of reality. By modifying the pluralistic perspective in this way, I think it is possible to see its compatibility with Christian belief. The remaining pages of this chapter will be devoted to exploring the possible configurations of this compatibility.

One place to begin is with the obvious development of the concept of God, together with an increasing inclusivism or universality of religious outlook, which characterizes the history of the Hebrew people as recorded in the Old Testament. There is a clear-cut progression from thinking of Jehovah as the God of the tribe or nation of Israel, in competition with other gods (those of Egypt and Canaan, especially), through a view of God as the only real God, with the others being "false gods" (roughly at the time of David and Soloman), to the high or 'radical' ethical monotheism of the major prophets (especially Isaiah). That Jehovah is the Lord of all humankind not only means that the Hebrew God is sovereign over all people, but that this God's love, grace, and justice is available to all, as well. Unfortunately, this is a truth which the Hebrew people continually forgot.

Returning to the statement of Jesus quoted at the beginning of this chapter, I should like at this juncture to make a suggestion concerning its interpretation in relation to the pluralistic posture outlined above. If one thinks of the revelatory and redeeming Word of God as focused or embodied in the Christ, Jesus of Nazareth, as the *principle* or basis upon which all true relationships to God are grounded, but which remains broader than this particular historical embodiment, then a richer interpretation of Jesus' statement is possible. The principle of God's sacrificial love, as expressed in Jesus Christ, *is* the Way, the Truth, and the Life, and no one can be redemptively related to God except through or by means of this principle.

All who live in meaningful and faithful relationship with God do so on the basis of this "Christ principle," whether they have heard of Jesus of Nazareth or not. This includes those who have heard and believed the Christian message as we think of it, as well as those who have encountered God's love and accepted it through whatever medium God has seen fit to use. This interpretation integrates Jesus' statement quoted above with his remarks recorded in Matthew 25, wherein he distinguishes between those who *claim* to live by his teachings but do not and those who *live* by his teachings without claiming to. This interpretation also fits Paul's remarks in Romans 2, about Gentiles who live according to God's principles even though they have not received any special revelation, either through the Hebrews or through Christians.

On the basis of this interpretation it is possible to acknowledge the possibility of true faith existing outside of the Christian religion while at the same time maintaining the universality and uniqueness of the "Christ principle" as revealed in Jesus of Nazareth. There may well be few who come to God by other means, but then when we get right down to it, setting aside "cultural Christians," narrow-minded distortions of the gospel, and shallow conversions, there are few who truly come to God through Christianity as well. In any case, those who come do so through Christ, whom Paul calls "the cosmic center" of God's creative and redemptive activity (see especially Colossians and Ephesians).

CULTURE AND CONVICTIONS

The significant role which our particular culture plays in determining our religious beliefs is often stressed by pointing out that had we been born in a different culture chances are extremely great that we would now be living according to the religion appropriate to that culture. The interpretive moves offered in the previous section were aimed at integrating this insight with the Christian claim to cruciality with respect to religious truth. In this section we shall come at this whole question from a different, more philosophical angle. The focus here will be on an understanding of religious beliefs that is broader than many Christians frequently admit, and on how such beliefs can be held to be true while at the same time acknowledging the possibility and necessity of remaining open to fresh truth.

To begin with, it is important to see that religious beliefs are more than mere sets of *propositions* that people assert as true about God, the world, and human life. Nor is religion simply a matter of living a certain *kind of life*, without any cognitive beliefs at all. When our religion really matters to us, it surely involves both what we *think* and how we *live*. Faith without works, as the Epistle of James teaches, is not dead because the two must go together, but because they are the same thing. To believe is to act and to act is to embody certain beliefs, even if they go unarticulated. It is helpful to call such all-pervasive and deeply rooted ways of thinking and behaving "convictions."[6]

A helpful way of understanding our belief system or "conviction sets" is in terms of our linguistic behavior. The activities and behavior patterns that comprise the way we live, both individually and in groups, are so inextricably interwoven into the things we say and the way we say them that in a deep sense our "speech acts" themselves are part and parcel of our way of being in the world. Speech is not arbitrary or optional phenomenon, for by it we enter into and continue to participate in the human world. Therefore, it is important to interpret our linguistic behavior—what we say, when, and how—as expressive of the deep structure of our lives. At the same time, coming from the other direction, it is equally important to realize that we learn to speak, both initially and as we continue to develop our convictions, through social interaction with others. We do not acquire our beliefs in a vacuum, but do so only as we participate in our common life with other persons.

All of this applies with equal force to religious convictions as well. Although ideally we come to internalize our religious beliefs individually, we are exposed to them initially through contact with others, and we continue to live them out through interaction with others. Thus there is a *social character* to our religious convictions that runs much deeper than many of us realize. And, of course, such socialization varies from culture to culture and from subgroup to subgroup. Not only do we have different religious conviction sets within differing cultures, but we have different ones within the same culture. Even within the same set we have significant as well as minute differences of belief and/or practice. Thus it is as complex as it is important to come to an understanding of why and how an individual alters his or her convictions, or "converts" from one set to another.

One helpful way to think about the question of truth with respect to differing and altering convictions is in terms of the notion of *perspectives.* We can think of conviction sets as simply a matter of point of view, with each person or group who holds a particular point of view aiming at the truth, namely at that perspective which is the *true* point of view. In this case it might be best to call this approach a "nonperspectivist" posture, in that it contends that perspectives are merely temporary disagreements resulting from differences of upbringing, data, or motivation, and that these will, or at least could, be dissolved through continued effort. At the opposite extreme is the "hard perspectivist" approach, which would hold that our differing points of view about things that matter the most are rooted so deeply in our biological, psychological, and social being that they can never be overcome. A mild form of hard perspectivism would be termed "relativism," while a more severe form, in which one argued that there is no true point of view, only perspectives, would be called "skepticism."

The stalemate that seems inevitably to arise whenever these nonperspective and hard perspective views square off is well-known. We have encountered it before in this particular exploration of the relation between religious faith and the various disciplines engaged in the search for truth. Generally speaking, Christians side with the nonperspectivist approach, partly to avoid the implications of relativism (to say nothing of skepticism!) and partly because they believe that God's point of view transcends all human perspectives. My own opinion at this juncture is that there is a more viable approach, one that constitutes a middle ground between hard perspectivism and nonperspectivism, that acknowledges the deep character of the differences among conviction sets, while affirming the value of continuing the search for truth without assuming that our (or my) set of convictions is necessarily the true one (God's). This third approach might be termed *"soft perspectivism."*

Soft perspectivism was the approach I touched on in the second section of chapter 3 when discussing relativism within the social sciences. The basic idea here is that to avoid the difficulties of the other two more extreme approaches, it is necessary to make a twofold distinction. On the one side, while acknowledging the depth and importance of our differing conviction sets, especially with respect to religious beliefs, it must be admitted that people do, in fact, alter their beliefs because they are convinced this alteration will bring them closer to the truth. Moreover, without this commitment to the possibility of overcoming, or at least minimizing, the effects of perspectivist influences, the hard perspectivist posture itself could not only *not* be *true*, it would not even be *intelligible*. All views *aim* at being true in a nonperspectivist sense; they all entail "universal intent"—even hard perspectivism!

On the other side, while acknowledging that there must in fact be an understanding of reality that transcends all perspectives (God's point of view), it must also be admitted that *no* particular human perspective, even that of the Christian, can claim to see or speak from that vantage point. Not only are our human interpretations of Christian truth, whether as individuals or groups, subject to error and distortion, but even the revelation of God in Christ itself is mediated "through a glass, darkly." That is to say, God's revelatory activity in the Incarnation, like divine action in the nation Israel, came in and through historical, societal, linguistic, and personal factors. The Judeo-Christian Scriptures as well were written in particular circumstances by a wide variety of writers for a number of distinct purposes. Neither Jesus Christ nor the Bible fell from heaven in a hermetically sealed bag, untouched by human hands.

Therefore, the revelation of God in Christ, the Word become flesh, can be taken as true in the sense that it is adequate or sufficient to reveal enough of God's character and love for redemptive purposes. But it must not be mistaken for a complete or exhaustive presentation of divine reality; it can be said to be true *qualitatively* but not quantitatively. Or, to change the terminology, the revelation of God in Christ can be said to be *absolute* qualitatively though not quantitatively. Thus, Christians must admit that there is always more to learn about God, the world, and human existence, even from cultures and conviction sets which seem quite different or opposed. In this way it is possible to hold that Christianity is true, while at the same time remain open to the possibility of fresh or further truth. An acknowledgement of the necessity of "universal intent" avoids the pitfalls of relativism; and a corresponding acknowledgement of human fallibility, as well as the mediated character of revelation, avoids the dangers of ethnocentricism and arrogance.

This way of putting the matter is simply a spelling-out of what in fact is already entailed in what we *mean* by a belief in everyday life. Clearly, to hold a belief is to be committed to its being true and to be able to give a rationale for it. At the same time, however, it goes without saying that our beliefs are subject to being incorrect, that we could, after all, be wrong. The possibility of being wrong is the price we pay for the possibility of being right. We are not speaking here of our degree of psychological certitude, but of the basic distinction between logical certainty and probability. Certainty can only be obtained in relation to closed, empty conceptual systems like mathematics and logic. Beliefs about reality only yield greater or lesser degrees of probability, no matter how certain we feel about them.

The posture I am recommending here is a *dialogical* one, similar to that which underlies the entire undertaking represented by this book. Its main concern is to create a basis for conversation and exploration between and among those who hold differing conviction sets, while at the same time allowing them to remain committed to their own belief systems as true. This posture is sometimes referred to as a "confessional stance,"[7] and it is of particular significance within a Christian context. According to it, a Christian can admit that cultural and other factors beyond his or her control have contributed to his or her particular conviction set and that there is much to learn from dialogue with persons of differing conviction sets, while yet maintaining that from where they stand at present, Christian faith seems to make the most sense.

My own way of expressing this posture is to say that although there is much truth in other religions—and I am still discovering this truth—at this point in my pilgrimage I find the most truth in Christianity. This does not imply that at any moment I am likely to "convert" out of my Christian faith, for it is deeply rooted and extremely meaningful to me in my daily life. It *does* imply, however, that I am open to God's continual activity in my life, illuminating ever more truth and deepening my understanding of what I already know. Moreover, I am motivated to share my faith with others, both within Christendom and outside it, not only because it is so meaningful and significant for me, but because it is possible that they may find it so for them as well. In short, others may grow closer to the truth as a result of our dialogue—*and* I, too, may grow closer to it in the same way. As a Christian, my responsibility is not to convince others that I am right, but simply to share and to serve.

Jesus and "Outsiders"

It is worth noting that those for whom Jesus reserved his most severe condemnation were the leaders of the religious orthodoxy of his day. Such an observation might well give those of us who profess to being deeply serious about our faith a great deal to think about. My focus of concern here, however, is on the fact that the converse of the above statement is also true: Jesus reserved his highest commendation for persons who in one way or another were "outside" the orthodox faith. More specifically, the people Jesus actually praised for their high quality of faith were frequently those who belonged to religions other than Judaism. In a time when Christians are increasingly challenged to rethink their traditional, exclusivist stand with respect to the relation between Christianity and other faiths, this is a very important consideration, indeed.

On the following pages I shall take up three instances in which Jesus is recorded as encountering persons of other religious persuasions, with an eye to tracing out the character of his posture toward them as it is revealed in the dialogue which takes place between them. I shall conclude with a brief discussion of the early church's attitude toward this issue as it is presented in the Book of Acts. My overall theme will be that Christians have much to learn from Jesus and the early church about the proper posture to be taken toward the relation between "true faith" and various cultural religious expressions thereof. There is an *inclusivist* tone, rather than an exclusivist one, to the way the "first Christians" addressed those of other faiths.

Let's begin with the story of Jesus and the Samaritan

woman at the well (John 4). There are several surprising features in Jesus' approach to this conversation, such as the fact that he actually entered into dialogue with a Samaritan, persons hated by the Jews as halfbreeds and heretics. In addition, Jesus was here talking with a woman in a public place, something that orthodox Jewish men were strongly encouraged to avoid. Then, too, there is the frank and engaging character of Jesus' speech, as well as the fact that he openly acknowledged his own need for water and asked for the woman's help in obtaining it. The most interesting feature of Jesus' stance toward this woman, however, is found in what he has to say about religion, truth, and real faith.

The Samaritans were descendants from Jews and Canaanites who had intermarried with people "imported" into Palestine by the Assyrians after having taken the Northern Kingdom captive in 721 B.C. As such, they were racially "impure" and held in disdain by Jews in both Galilee and Judea." No self-respecting Jew even traveled through Samaria, let alone spoke seriously and openly with a Samaritan. These were the untouchables, the "Niggers" of Jesus' day. This is what gives so much force to Jesus' story of the "Good Samaritan," for in it the specifically orthodox priest and Levite passed by the needy person, while the much despised Samaritan took the time and trouble to become involved.

What is of specific interest to our purposes, however, is the way in which Jesus treats the religious differences between Jews and Samaritans. The two most distinctive features of the Samaritan faith were their belief that Mt. Gerizim, not Jerusalem, was the proper place to worship, and their limiting the Scriptures to the first five books of the Old Testament. In nearly all other respects, they were essentially similar to Judaism. Thus it is clear that they did not regard themselves as inferior to Jews, but thought of their own faith as the true embodiment of God's activity in the history of Israel. In fact, it is fair to say that the Samaritans thought of themselves as more orthodox than the Jews, because they had not added recent events, practices, and writings to their religion.

Now in this context the woman said to Jesus, in effect, "You Jews say that Jerusalem is the proper place to worship Jehovah, while we Samaritans say that Mt. Gerizim is. Which view is the true one?" It is not immediately clear whether she was introducing this "theological issue" to divert the conversation away from more personal matters or out of a sincere desire to know the truth. The fact that Jesus took her question seriously might well indicate that the latter possibility is the more likely. In any case, it is Jesus' reply that is of special interest for us. For he said, essentially, "The place of worship is not of primary importance. It is time to transcend these kinds of differences. God is a spirit and as such cannot be limited to location. Those who worship God must do so in spirit and in truth." In other words, true worship is a *qualitative* matter, not a quantitative one.

What is striking to me here is that Jesus did not bother to set the woman "right" religiously, nor spell out the theological differences between orthodoxy and heterodoxy. In fact, he actually set such matters aside as irrelevant to the central concern of religious belief. Moreover, he did not, either here nor *anywhere*, offer his own set of "religious" doctrines and practices as a replacement for these traditional but now outmoded belief systems. He simply went to the heart of the matter, stressing quality of faith and presenting himself, God's special representative, as the proper focus of true faith. It is important to note, too, that he tied his comments to her acknowledged belief in a coming Messiah, thereby establishing a common basis for dialogue and better understanding.

Things get even more interesting when we consider Jesus' encounter with the Roman centurion (Luke 7). Here is a person who is ostensibly a "pagan," a worshiper of Roman gods, perhaps even of Caesar himself. And yet, those who described him to Jesus did so in glowing terms, stressing his *sincerity* of faith and his significant *deeds* of charity toward the Jewish people, in spite of the fact that he was in their midst as a representative of an oppressive military force. These people were not particularly uptight about specific religious labels, but were more concerned with the concrete expression of a person's faith, for as Jesus had said, "By their fruits you shall know them."

The issue here is not whether one earns redemption by good works or receives it by grace and faith alone. Clearly, no one "earns" God's mercy and love. The issue is, rather, whether authentic religion has as much to do with traditional, cultural manifestation as it does with integrity and commitment to the degree of truth one has received. Jesus' response would seem to indicate that it is the latter that counts. The centurion's servant was ill, and he asked Jesus to heal him simply by revealing his understanding of the parallel between political and spiritual authority. Jesus marveled at his deep insight and uttered the following amazing comment to his disciples: "I have not found so great faith in all of Israel." The centurion's servant was healed on the basis of the *faith* of his master, even though neither of them was a Jew nor a follower of Jesus.

A third, and perhaps even more significant, incident is the encounter between Jesus and the Syro-Phoenician woman (Matthew 15). Jesus and his disciples were on "vacation" in a region that lay outside of the dominant influence of traditional Jewish faith. He was not engaged in any specific preaching or healing ministry at the time. All at once this woman began to beseech his help on behalf of her sick daughter. The disciples urged Jesus to send her away, partly because they were not "on duty" at this time and partly because she was clearly not of the proper religious persuasion. But the woman persisted and finally succeeded in getting Jesus' attention. Then followed one of the most surprising and enlightening dialogues in the entire Scriptures.

Jesus began by asking a question that at first blush might seem extremely racist. He asked, "Is it not true that the nourishment of divine love is reserved for God's children, the especially chosen people of Israel, and is not available to the dogs, the unchosen outsiders?" In my opinion it does not take a great deal of reflection to see that Jesus is employing *ironic humor* in order to discern the quality of the woman's faith. His irony is actually twofold, against the Jews who consistently referred to Gentiles as "dogs" on the one hand and against those who saw themselves as God's "special people" on the other. There is even a special edge to his question that is aimed at his disciples. This move on Jesus' part makes it plain that in his view, true faith has nothing to do with which socioreligious group one belongs to, whether inside orthodoxy or outside of it.

The woman was quick to reply in kind, thereby indicating *both* that she understood the good-natured tone of Jesus' question (perhaps from a smile or twinkle in his eye) *and* that she understood that sincerity and integrity are what really matter when one comes to God. She said, "True enough, but even the 'dogs' hustle after the leftovers that the [ungrateful?] 'children' don't appropriate." Jesus was truly amazed at the depth of her spiritual insight and responded by praising her faith and healing her daughter, even though she most likely knew next to nothing of the actual beliefs of the Hebrews and even less of what we would call the main beliefs of Christianity. Jesus' posture toward people of true faith, irrespective of their religious background and persuasion, was an *inclusive* one, not an exclusive one. He freely shared the healing love of God with whoever sincerely sought it, with no compunction against calling them "people of faith."

It is extremely interesting to pursue this theme in relation to the attitudes of the leaders of the early church, especially Paul and Peter. The first Christians were, of course, Jewish in background, and they saw their Christian faith as an extension and fulfillment of their Judaism. Moreover, they continued in their exclusivist assumption that the gospel of Jesus Christ was meant for Jews alone. Paul challenged this assumption, insisting that God's love cannot be restricted by religious and/or genetic boundaries, and thereby gave rise to the central drama of the early church's development. The ensuing conflict came to a head at the council of Jerusalem recorded in Acts 15 where the church decided in Paul's favor that "God is no respector of persons."

It is instructive to conclude our present investigation with a consideration of the dynamics of Peter's personal struggle with this issue, presented in Acts 10. Peter was on the roof, waiting for supper to be prepared, when he had a vision of a large sheet full of "unclean," nonkosher animals being lowered to him from above. He recognized the voice of God (or perhaps Jesus) saying to him, "Go ahead and eat." Now Peter is well-known for his quick and vehement reaction in situations where commitment was involved—he was nearly always the first to affirm or deny what was at issue. In this case he clearly discerned the meaning of what was said and who it was that was saying it. And he replied, "Not so, Lord! I have never eaten anything unclean and I'm not about to start now."

This pattern was repeated two more times before Peter began to weaken. Then the servants of Cornelius, a Roman centurion who was seeking the truth, arrived at the door and Peter began to grasp the implications of his vision. At the church council in Jerusalem he testified that God's spirit had made it clear to him that persons of other faiths, "outsiders," were not excluded from God's love as revealed in Christ—though at one point Paul indicates that Peter was once again guilty of turning his back to the truth. Paul's letter to the Galatians indicates the struggle the early church continued to have with those legalists who insisted that Gentiles must become Jews in order to participate fully in God's grace.

My point is simply that it is entirely *possible* our world may have arrived at a similar point in time with respect to the relation between the Christian religion and those of other faiths as Peter and Paul faced in regard to the relation between the fulfillment of Judaism and Gentiles of deep commitment. It is important that we maintain a posture which is open to fresh truth, that we do not find ourselves saying to God, "Not so, Lord!" The issues here are as complex as they are significant, and I am not recommending a simple-minded inclusivist posture which would blandly ignore the many differences among various religious faiths. However, as we Christians learn more and more about other cultures and traditions, and as we come to know persons who actually practice different religions with a deep spiritual commitment to divine truth, it is imperative that we concentrate on the *quality* of faith and life and not on external considerations. After all, Jesus consistently set aside religious differences when it came to the authenticity of an individual's relation to spiritual truth, and even Paul and Peter came to see that the love of God cannot be limited by traditional distinctions between those who are "chosen" and those who are not.

Suggested Reading

Hick, John. *Truth and Dialogue in World Religions.* Philadelphia: Westminister, 1974.

Newbigin, Leslie. *The Finality of Christ.* Atlanta: John Knox, 1969.

Niebuhr, H. R. *The Meaning of Revelation.* New York: MacMillan, 1941.

Noss, John. *Man's Religions.* New York: MacMillan, 1963.

Smith, Huston. *The Religions of Man.* New York: Harper & Row, 1958.

Tillich, Paul. *Christianity and the Encounter of the World Religions.* New York: Columbia Univ. Press, 1963.

A Fresh Start: 7
Reasons of the Heart

WE HAVE NOW ARRIVED at the long-advertised (perhaps *over-advertised!*) chapter 7. In it, I shall try to reward the reader's patience at being asked repeatedly to wait for a more thorough response to the various issues discussed along the way. The bother has been that the standard way of setting the problems up is almost invariably rooted in what seem to me to be wrong-headed, if unarticulated, presuppositions at the deepest level. Thus, the difficulties could not be squarely faced until our presuppositions could be shifted, but it was not possible to introduce such a shift until the need for doing so was clearly apparent. Now that we have reviewed and engaged some of the major issues in the dialogue between Christian faith and the main areas of concern within the academy, we are in a position to propose a new way of coming at them which, I hope, will render the ongoing dialogue more fruitful.

As we noted in chapter 1, Pascal, a Christian philosopher from around Descartes' time, suggested that the main difficulty in dealing with the relation between faith and rationality lies in coming to an understanding of the fact that "the heart has reasons which reason knows not of." I do not think Pascal was advocating a complete split between reason and faith, for after all he *did* call the "reasons of the heart" *reasons*. In the pages that follow I shall sketch out an approach to understanding and reorienting the basis upon which the dialogue between rationality and religious belief takes place that seeks to make sense of Pascal's insight without sacrificing either side of the dialogue to the other.[1] In the final chapter we shall return briefly to the issues discussed in the previous chapters from the perspective provided by this fresh approach by way of suggesting how the dialogue might be continued.

REALMS AND DIMENSIONS

Many of the basic presuppositions of Western thought can be summarized under the heading "critical philosophy." Ever since the time of Plato, but especially in modern times (since Descartes and the British Empiricists), certain assumptions concerning the nature of reality, language, and knowledge have been operative. In the three sections of this chapter I shall take up each of these latter three notions, first in terms of their treatment by critical philosophy and then from a fresh, "postcritical" perspective. Nearly all of the issues we have encountered thus far have arisen because those working in the various disciplines comprising the academic enterprise have adopted the presuppositions of critical philosophy on a "no questions asked" basis. It is high time we asked some fundamental questions about these presuppositions. The first area of the critical posture that must be examined is that of our understanding of the structure of *reality*. Although the limitations of space, to say nothing of the limitations of our knowledge, will not permit a full-scale treatment of metaphysics, perhaps I can show what I take to be the chief areas of difficulty and how they can be helpfully altered.

There are three aspects of the traditional, critical approach to the nature of reality that need to be focused. The first is its *atomistic* character. The general assumption of modern Western thought concerning reality is that it comes in variously sized "chunks" which can be identified, separated, and analyzed independently of one another. It is commonly assumed that any given phenomenon (a person, place, thing, or idea) consists of essential constituents out of which it is made and which can be clearly distinguished through rational analysis. In short, the whole is equal to the sum of its parts, and every whole is made up of parts. Thus all forms of physical reality (animal, vegetable, mineral), together with all aspects of human life (individuals, groups, ideas, activities), exist as, and can be studied in terms of, the individual parts which comprise them.

I do not wish to suggest that atomistic analysis is of no value in our understanding of reality. After all, throughout our entire discussion, as well as in this current examination of critical thought, we are relying heavily upon it. What I do wish to propose, however, is that the unreflective assumption that reality *itself*, rather than one particular way of thinking of it, must consist of such molecular constructs is highly questionable. There are ways of thinking about reality developed in other cultures which do not make this assumption and which serve the people of those cultures quite well. I am thinking here of Eastern modes of thought, as well as those of Africans and the American Indians. Moreover, not only are there other ways of thinking developed in the West (not all philosophers, scientists, artists, etc. buy into the critical approach), but it remains and may well continue to remain unclear just what the "proper" and/or "complete" analysis of a given aspect of reality might be. In a word, we have no criterion, and in principle may not be able to devise one, for knowing when we have the right parts or all of the parts of a phenomenon.

A second and related feature of critical Western thought is its assumption concerning the possibility and value of *"objectivity."* In every area of cognitive endeavor we are constantly told to strive to be objective, to describe and rely upon the facts alone. True understanding is said to be nonsubjective (impersonal) and "value-free." Now clearly, this is a praiseworthy goal, especially with respect to overcoming individual bias, ethnocentrism, and historical limitations. But when it is carried to an extreme so as to become a "dogma," it becomes counterproductive to the cognitive enterprise. Not only can we never actually achieve "absolute objectivity," but there is serious question as to whether the concept has any meaning in this sense. After all, as Heisenberg's principle of indeterminacy has shown, any knowledge of any aspect of reality is achieved through some form of interaction, thus altering that reality, or better yet creating altogether a fresh one. In addition, there are many thinkers who have made an excellent case for the idea that there are no "facts" as such, that all facts exist only as part of a larger pattern formed by some theory or other. Without a theory that tells us which observations and so forth are "relevant," the concept of a fact makes no sense. All facts are "theory-laden."[2]

Thirdly, critical philosophy has from the outset operated on the assumption that reality is comprised of, and can only be understood in terms of, various levels or realms. This *"realm-ism"* is generally dualistic in character, the theory being that above this temporal and material world there is a spiritual world which is eternal and more important. We took up this dualism, and the modern denial of it, in chapter 4, so I will not repeat that discussion here. Suffice it to say that this realm-ism, whether in its positive, vertical form or its negative, horizontal form, goes hand-in-hand with atomism. For it, too, assumes that reality consists of separate parts which can be distinguished and examined *independently* of one another. The chief difficulty here, as before, is that of finding agreement with respect to how many and which parts or realms there are, as well as that of agreeing on a criterion for distinguishing one from the other.

Now a word about the implications of the critical approach to reality for our understanding of religious belief in general and Christian faith in particular. Frequently it has been assumed that only philosophy and science aim at being—and can be—objective; that religion, along with art and public morality, is essentially subjective and necessarily biased in character. Prior to the Modern era, and occasionally within it (especially among fundamentalists), there have been those who maintained that religion, too, yields absolute, objective truth, much like that of science and philosophy. But agreement as to what this "ultimate truth" consists of has remained impossible. So we are forced to choose between thinking of religious faith as "objective" without being able to establish it as such on the one hand and accepting it as "subjective" without a criterion for distinguishing one faith from another on the other hand. Thus the split between reason and faith represented in various versions of Christian existentialism.

The atomism of Modern critical thought has driven the friends and foes of religious reality alike to analyze it in terms of its constituent parts. Its friends generally seek to isolate some particular aspect of human experience, such as the feeling of dependency, the miracles of Jesus, the classical "proofs" of God's existence, and so on, as specific instances of or evidence for spiritual reality and truth. Its foes usually seek to reduce all such aspects to other, naturalistic factors, thereby rejecting the possibility of a "higher" reality. Religious experience and/or revelation is either denied outright or reinterpreted humanistically. The only alternative to this reductionism is to view religious experience and/or revelation as a clear-cut *intrusion* of the divine into the natural realm. The trouble is, the only criteria that can be offered for identifying these intrusions are either *human* and *natural* ones (agreed upon "facts", logical arguments, and so on) or they turn out to be nothing but the bias or "say-so" of one person (or group) or another.

My own proposal is that we set aside the assumptions of critical thought, thereby opening the way for a more viable posture with respect to the nature of reality. To begin with, it is essential that we think of reality as *experienced reality,* doing away with the notion that it exists independently of our participation in it. This is not to say that we create our own reality, but rather that the only reality with which we can possibly have to do (think of, talk about, study) is that with which we *interact*. Moreover, this interaction with experienced reality is never in terms of isolated parts which can be dealt with or understood apart from one another. Rather, it takes place in a "thickly" woven environmental fabric. Thus, while it may be helpful for specific purposes to analyze various features of reality as abstracted from their relation to other aspects, we must always remember that this is indeed an *abstraction*. Reality only has meaning for us, hence the *concept* of reality only has meaning for us, *because* and *as* we interact with it, both physically and sociolinguistically.[3]

Viewing reality in this way not only helps to overcome the limitations of atomism, but also does away with the "cult" of objectivity. For now we realize that there is no possibility, let alone necessity, of obtaining an absolutely objective description or understanding of reality. Reality and our understanding of it (interaction with it) only exist, *for us,* symbiotically; they are defined in terms of one another. And even to say that the expression "for us" implies a reality which exists independently of us is *to speak of* and thus in some sense interact with that reality, thereby showing that it is *not* independent of us. We can, of course, still distinguish between descriptions and evaluations of specific aspects of the world which are objective and subjective but not in any absolute sense. Rather, given a concrete context created by certain agreed-upon tasks and ways of speaking, we can determine the *degree* to which someone (including ourselves) may be thinking or acting in a manner that is irrelevant or contrary to our common purposes. Moreover, without these common commitments and skills we would be completely unable to obtain any knowledge at all—or even place a shared value on objectivity itself.

The "realm-ism" generally associated with critical thought needs to be replaced with a view which understands reality as comprised of simultaneously interpenetrating *dimensions* arranged according to a hierarchy of richness and comprehensiveness.[4] This statement is rather a mouthful, so let me take some time to analyze it. Rather than thinking of reality as consisting of separate realms, or of just one horizontal level, I would suggest that the relationship among the various major areas of experienced reality is better thought of as similar to that among the spatiotemporal dimensions in which we live. These dimensions, up-down, right-left, near-far, and so on, interpenetrate each other in such a way that whatever happens or is done in one affects what takes place in the others, and vice versa. Further, the structure of this multidimensional reality is hierarchical in the sense that the more comprehensive and rich dimensions are mediated in and through those that are less so. Thus each contains yet is limited by those beneath it, each is encountered only through those comprising and mediating it, but each cannot be reduced to or exhaustively accounted for in terms of the others.

Perhaps a more concrete example is in order at this juncture. Imagine people watching swimmers from a bridge over a river. All at once a small child is seen floating face-down in the water. One observer offers a description of the situation strictly in terms of the physics involved: so many pounds of protoplasm floating in a certain chemical solution at such-and-such an angle and rate, etc. Another person (clearly a more normal or humane person) describes the situation quite differently—as a moral context demanding immediate action, etc. —and behaves accordingly. Still a third person might offer an aesthetic description of the scene, another a personal account (the child's parent, perhaps), and so on. Finally, another person may later offer a religious account, speaking of the sanctity of human life as an aspect of God's created order, of the problem of evil, or of the will of God in relation to human responsibility (including their own).

The major thing to notice here is that none of these differing accounts or the dimensions of human experience they embody actually conflict with one another. Each is true and perhaps valuable in its own way. Nonetheless, they are arranged according to a hierarchy of comprehensiveness and richness in which each successive account depends upon the previous ones while at the same time goes beyond them.

There is nothing incorrect about the purely physical account, *per se;* it just does not go far enough. The moral point of view and the personal perspective are "deeper" or "broader." And the religious dimension is not "above" or "beyond" the others in the sense of being separable from them; rather, it is mediated *in and through* them. The physical context is necessary for, yet not exhaustive of, the moral one; the moral is part of but not all of the personal dimension, and so on. Finally, the religious dimension is *discerned* as richer and more comprehensive by means of interaction within the other dimensions.

The overall advantage of this dimensional understanding of reality for our view of the nature of religious experience is that it enables us to speak of revelation and/or spiritual awareness as *contiguous* with the rest of experience without its being reducible to it. Instead of conceiving of divine activity as an intrusion into the human and natural worlds, we can now see it as being in basic harmony with them. In addition to harmonizing God's redemptive activity with the original created order (this *is* God's world, after all), this approach opens up the possibility of developing criteria for authentic discernment of spiritual reality which are not subjective and circular on the one hand, nor "merely" humanistic or naturalistic on the other. Even though agreement about aesthetic reality is difficult to get and define, it is not impossible in a rough-and-ready sense. The same may be true for our discernment of divine reality if we can get beyond traditional, realmistic presuppositions.

FUNCTION AND METAPHOR

The second main aspect of the traditional Western, or critical, posture which needs dismantling is its approach to the nature of *linguistic expression.* Once again, it must be noted that the presuppositions upon which this approach has been based have remained prereflective and unarticulated until Modern times. The vast majority of philosophers, as well as theologians, have devoted their energies to thinking and talking about reality, truth, and value without ever turning their attention directly to the medium through and by means of which they carry on the entire enterprise, namely language. Beginning with the turn of the present century, however, there has been a great deal of interest in what language is and how it works. As a result, there has been a parallel increase of interest in the nature and function of religious and theological discourse, or "God-talk." In my opinion, this latter concern has been stalemated by the presuppositions underlying the dominant perspective of the former, more general concern with language. Let me explain.

Throughout the history of Western thought there has existed an unspoken assumption that the primary, if not the only, purpose of language is to *represent* reality, whether physical or mental. At the base of this assumption lies the presupposition that words function as *names* for objects, thoughts, and qualities. When these words are put together in sentences, it was supposed, the result is a linguistic picture of the facts or state of affairs being talked about. This basic approach began to be articulated in Modern times, and was powerfully focused in the works of such thinkers as Bertrand Russell, the Vienna Circle, the early Wittgenstein, and A. J. Ayer. This "picture theory" of meaning, together with its implications for theology and religious belief, was discussed in chapter 4, but will bear further consideration here.

If the words "triangle" and "square" are taken as names for these two objects, respectively, △ and □, and the word "above" is taken as the name for a potential relationship between them, then the statement "The triangle is above the square" can be viewed as a grammatical or logical representation (picture) of this state of affairs: △. On the surface, this would seem to be the way all language functions, and this conclusion is reinforced by our own experience with learning foreign languages (vocabulary lists, etc.) and in talking with small children ("See Mary," "See Mary run," etc.). Moreover, we imagine that preliterate peoples speak "primitive" languages composed by stringing word-names together ("You Jane," "Me Tarzan," etc.). According to such a view, the *meaning* of utterances, and of all speech, lies in their representing facts, while their *truth* (or falseness) is a function of whether or not they picture the facts correctly—thus, the verifiability criterion of meaning and truth discussed in chapter 4.

On the common sense level, the purpose of language would seem to be the transfer of information, and communications "experts" (especially computer theorists and linguists) often speak as if this were the case. In addition, it is generally assumed that scientific language represents the highest form of this mode of communication because it is the most precise and objective. It is easy to see, as well, why religious and theological language should be thought to have as its primary purpose the transfer of information about divine reality as clearly and accurately as possible. Thus, God-talk is generally thought of as providing pictures or representations of how things are with God and with God's relation to the world. Such a conclusion leads, however, to the difficulties of verifiability for both meaningfulness and truth, which we took up in chapter 4.

It was primarily the later work of Wittgenstein[5] that enabled philosophers and theologians to see that the picture theory of the meaning of language simply will not do. The fundamental reason it will not do, and this point is of inestimable significance, is that on closer inspection it becomes perfectly clear that the *main* purpose of language (let alone its *only* purpose) is *not* the transference of information. On the contrary, language serves as a means of communication of and about a vastly wide variety of things, including but going well beyond passing information and/or representing facts. We invite, warn, propose, speculate, tell stories and jokes, pray, curse, sing, question, give orders, plan, and repent; none of these linguistic activities can properly be called "picturing facts."

More importantly, the representative function of language

only takes on meaning from its place within the wider contexts of one of the foregoing activities. People do not just go
around blurting out "facts," but they do pass along information as a means of accomplishing a given task, such as those
mentioned above. We do not say things like "It's cold in
here," "The road turns left," or "I did it and I am sorry" for
their own sake, but to communicate at a more primordial
level, the level of everyday life. As Wittgenstein might have
put it, linguistic meaning is a function of use in context.
There are many more, as well as deeper, uses of speech than
transferring information, although this, too, has its place.

This more tolerant, *functional* way of viewing language and
meaningfulness calls attention to the inextricable relationship
between language, action, and reality. Speech is, after all, a
kind of action, since we actually *do* things with words (such as
apologize, promise, object, and so on). And action, or the lack
thereof, can be every bit as expressive as speech, given the
right context. In addition, both speech and action are *constituents* of reality, rather than mere descriptions of or reactions to
it. Thus it is that anyone who pays attention to how small
children *actually* acquire their mother tongue will see that it is
not a matter of learning vocabulary first, as names of things,
etc., and then making the proper application in order to convey information. Nor do preliterate people speak "primitive"
languages, for even aborigines have highly complex languages. Words are employed by both children and aborigines, as well as civilized adults, to get jobs done; thus their
established and conventional meanings arise out of use, and
vice versa.

The further and significant ramifications of this revolution
in the philosophy of language for what might be termed the
"metaphoric mode" are especially worth noting. It is possible
to make a case[6] for the primordial nature of metaphoric
speech, including analogy, parable, and onomatopoeia in relation to so-called "literal" speech. It is fairly easy to show
that what we regard as literal words and statements are actu-

ally expressions which were once metaphoric in character. In other words, there are only two kinds of speech, live metaphors and dead ones (even the term "literal" is a dead metaphor, as a quick check with a good dictionary will indicate). Since so-called literal expressions were once metaphoric, it follows that the metaphoric mode is more basic. Language arises out of our primordial interaction with the world, both physical and social, and at this level the connection between the world, speech, and ourselves is more integral than our more precise and articulated speech would lead us to believe. It would seem that religion itself would arise from this more primordial level of human existence and that God-talk would have its deepest grounding in the metaphoric mode.

The standard objection to this way of thinking is to claim that since increased precision brings increased understanding, it follows that nonmetaphoric speech is preferable to metaphoric, especially in theology. The difficulty with this move, as Wittgenstein showed, is that precision is neither possible nor necessary as an *ideal* for communication. It is not possible because no matter how many refinements we make, contexts will always arise or be imagined in which further precision is advisable. There is no such thing as absolute precision, only *significant precision vis-à-vis the context and purposes at hand*. That precision is not necessary to meaningful communication can be seen from the fact that, if it were, no one would ever be able to learn language. Precision moves by degrees from less to more, but one must start where one is, with what communication can be established, and become more precise as is needed. In short, we must be able to understand one another at some level to effect greater precision; not every word or statement can be explained in terms of others or we would never get started.

The power of the metaphoric mode as a means of communication resides in its ability to speak of more than one aspect or level of experienced reality simultaneously. Although the risk of miscommunication because of ambiguity is always present, it is precisely this ambiguity that gives metaphor its power and significance. For certain tasks, like those of exact measurement, it is desirable to eliminate as much ambiguity and vagueness as is required by the context. For other tasks, however, especially when speaking about the great values and mysteries of life, it may at times be advisable to preserve ambiguity and vagueness so as not to eliminate the meaning thereof. In the song, "Georgia on My Mind," for instance, it is unclear whether the person is singing about his place of origin or a woman—and this ambiguity is the heart of the value and significance of the song. Or, to take another example, in cases requiring great diplomacy, it may not be advisable to be too precise because doing so might forfeit the very possibility of agreement.

When this understanding of the nature of language is brought to bear on the question of the meaning of religious and theological discourse, the results are as exciting as they are astounding. It is safe to say that the vast majority of Christian thinking about the function of God-talk has been predicated on the assumption, borrowed from Western philosophy, that the chief end of language is to transfer information about reality by representing states of affairs. Thus, the primary purpose of religious discourse is to convey knowledge about God and the world by picturing what might be called "theological facts." There are, of course, some notable exceptions to this way of thinking, such as Aquinas' notion of "analogy of proportionality"[7] and Paul Tillich's concept of God-talk as "symbolic,"[8] but these have not carried us very far. Aquinas fell back on literal or factual language when dealing with the Scriptures and teachings of the church, while Tillich so diffused the notion of symbol as to render it next to useless.

As I indicated in chapter 4, I believe there is great promise in pursuing the insights of the later Wittgenstein, especially as they apply to metaphoric speech, in our efforts to understand the nature and function of God-talk. First, the stress

Wittgenstein placed on the inextricable interconnections among language, action, and reality casts a good deal of light on the relationship between Christian faith and life, especially when viewed from the perspective provided by our analysis in the previous chapter of the convictional and social basis of all religious belief. For too long Christians have thought of theological language as simply a representation of objective, "metaphysical facts" or of subjective, personal commitment. It is important that we understand that our talk of God is part of an entire fabric woven out of our shared experience and common activity. In an extremely significant sense, our speech about and to God *is* our faith, not just a representation of it—and our way of embodying faith is also an *expression* of it. Faith without action is not faith at all, and faithful action is what faith is all about.

Second, the fact that the metaphoric mode enables us to speak of two aspects of experience simultaneously provides a very helpful way of thinking about religious discourse. The twofold character of much biblical and theological language, as explored by Ian Ramsey and discussed in chapter 4, is largely explained by this way of understanding metaphoric speech. Further, it can be seen that this mode of expression is uniquely appropriate for speaking about richer and more comprehensive dimensions of reality as they are mediated in and through less rich and comprehensive dimensions. For this mediational dynamic is also characteristic of the metaphysical mode of speech, since with it we speak of one aspect of experienced reality *in, through, and by* speaking of another. This multidimensional nature of metaphor is the mainspring of the very possibility of language itself, since without it we would have to start from scratch when talking about something other than what we had already talked about. And by means of it we are enabled to speak about those dimensions of our world, such as the moral, aesthetic, and religious, which are both immanent in and transcendent of the physical dimension. Thus, to speak of theological language as "mere" metaphor is to betray a shallow understanding of both speech and life. [9]

Third, it is certainly significant that Jesus' main means of speaking about God, the kingdom, and faith was the metaphoric mode. Basically, Jesus was a storyteller. Not only did he continually refer to himself as the "light of the world," the "bread of life," etc., but he likened God to a shepherd, master, father, mother hen, and servant. Moreover, when speaking of the kingdom and of our relation to it, Jesus consistently employed analogies and parables. This can be said to be the most characteristic feature of his entire ministry. It is important for Christians to reflect on the significance of this point for understanding the nature of religious and theological language. Jesus did not write at all, nor did he teach in the form of scientific or philosophical expositions. Such analytic and systematic modes are appropriate as a part of our *reflection on* God's revelation, but they are not to be confused *with* that disclosure. The Incarnation was in a *person* who lived and spoke in concrete terms, albeit in such a manner as to mediate spiritual reality and truth. Thus Jesus can be said to be, both in life and teaching, the "Metaphor of God."

The great advantage of the metaphoric mode's "open texture" for understanding the function of religious language is twofold. On the one hand, its two-dimensional ambiguity creates a *space*, an "existential arena," wherein the hearer can encounter the truth, yet without being "force-fed." This space preserves and respects the hearer's freedom and dignity. At the same time, on the other hand, this double-edged quality of metaphor invites and entices the hearer to step into the space it creates, if he or she sincerely seeks the truth. Thus it emphasizes and urges individual responsibility and commitment. Over and over again we see Jesus creating this space between himself and the persons he meets by answering a question with yet another question, by telling a parable, or by engaging in "offbeat," seemingly irrelevant behavior. His metaphorical activity always *engages* them at the concrete

level where they live *and encourages* them to see or walk forward to a richer understanding and commitment.[10]

THE EXPLICIT AND THE TACIT

The final area of Western, critical thought in which a revolution is required is that of epistemology, the theory of
knowledge. At least since Plato, it has generally been assumed that a belief or an assumption cannot qualify as
knowledge until its meaning and rationale can be fully articulated. While this theory of knowledge is quite helpful in
many respects, it is equally pernicious when carried to an
extreme—and most philosophers (and theologians) have
fallen into the trap of carrying it to the extreme. The theory is
clearly necessary in certain contexts, as when someone claims
to know something but is completely unable to give any indi-
cation what is known or how it is known. But, since there is
no such thing as "absolute" clarity or proof, and since all
explanations and justifications must come to an end in order
for them to function as such, it is equally clear that there is
something wrong with the above account of the nature of
knowledge. For it offers us a definition of knowledge that
makes it unattainable.

The religious counterpart to this epistemological difficulty
is seen in the dichotomy which has arisen between those who
defend Christian belief as true because it provides objective,
absolute knowledge about God and human life on the one
side and those who insist that it fails to do so on the other
side. It is important to see that both sides in this debate accept full articulation as the requirement for knowledge; they
then disagree about whether this requirement has been or
can be met. Both seem right and both seem wrong. The trick
is to find some way of thinking about knowledge that renders
it both attainable (nonabsolute) and reliable (nonsubjective). I
offer the following model as a substitute for that used by
traditional philosophical and theological thinkers.[11]

It is helpful to think of human experience as comprised of

two dimensions, the *awareness* dimension and the *activity* dimension. The former has as its poles *subsidiary* and *focal* awareness. In every situation we are aware of some aspects focally and of others subsidiarily. You are now, or were, subsidiarily aware that your feet are in shoes and that I am using written symbols to communicate my ideas to you. When buying your shoes, or when simply reading these words for their meaning, you were focally aware of these things. We always attend *from* some aspects of our environment *to* others, even though generally what is focal can become subsidiary in a different context, and vice versa. The poles of the activity dimension of experience are *conceptual* activity and *bodily* activity. Although there may be no hard and fast line between these two, we can generally distinguish them from each other. Doing math problems in one's head and running the hundred-yard dash are significantly different activities. Moreover, from birth onward we tend to move from bodily activity toward conceptual activity. Our thought life is in some basic way dependent on our physical life.

Now, when these two major dimensions of human existence intersect, yet a third, more complex, dimension emerges—that of *cognitivity*. The interaction between focal awareness and conceptual activity gives rise to one pole of this cognitivity dimension, while that between subsidiary awareness and bodily activity gives rise to the other. The first may be termed "explicit knowing" and the second "tacit knowing." Explicit knowing is essentially what we in the West have called knowledge itself, involving the isolation of particulars, precise definitions, objective descriptions, and the articulation of a rationale. Tacit knowing, on the other hand, is a range of experience which generally has been denied cognitive status, being relegated to the vague and untrustworthy domain of the "subjective," because it is said to be comprised of feelings, values, commitments, and generalizations. The diagram on the next page should be helpful in suggesting the interrelations among these three dimensions or spectra:

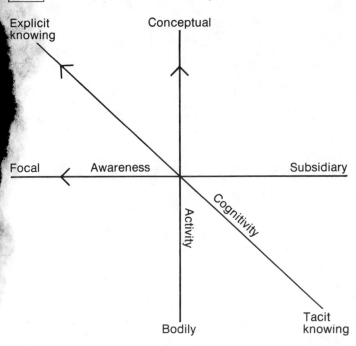

My primary proposal is that we broaden our understanding of cognitivity to include the tacit range as well as the explicit. This move is the one poets, mystics, romanticists, existentialists, and the like have been urging (albeit without much clarity or success) throughout the history of Western thought. It simply will not do, however, to define cognitivity exclusively in terms of explicit knowing, only to find that all other knowing important to human *living* has been given inferior status. What must be done, rather, is to conceive of, indeed to see that at the concrete level we already *do* conceive of, knowledge as having a tacit as well as an explicit range. Particular bodily skills such as walking, riding bicycles, and speaking, for instance, are examples of knowledge that cannot be fully articulated or taught by passing along formulae from one person to the next. This sort of knowing is *demon-*

licit
wing

ceptual

ness

ary

vity

ving

vity

ly

My primary proposal is that we broaden our understanding of cognitivity to include the tacit range as well as the
explicit. This move is the one poets, mystics, romanticists,
existentialists, and the like have been urging (albeit without
much clarity or success) throughout the history of Western
thought. It simply will not do, however, to define cognivity
exclusively in terms of explicit knowing, only to find that all
other knowing important to human *living* has been given inferior status. What must be done, rather, is to conceive of,
indeed to see that at the concrete level we already *do* conceive
of, knowledge as having a tacit as well as an explicit range.
Particular bodily skills such as walking, riding bicycles, and
speaking, for instance, are examples of knowledge that cannot be fully articulated or taught by passing along formulae
from one person to the next. This sort of knowing is *demon-*

strated rather than formulated or explained; it is *caught* rather than taught. And it is as common and familiar as everyday life.

Other, more complex and significant examples of tacit knowing are such things as knowing our primary language and knowing persons. The mother tongue is not and cannot be taught by explicit precept, definitions, grammatical rules, and the like, for the simple reason that prior to speaking this language no other language exists in which to express such formulae. By the age of six, however, nearly every child has essentially acquired the totality of a highly complex symbol system, with the aid of little if any explicit instruction. In like manner, we all come to a knowledge of other persons that far exceeds, both in depth and in breadth, any list of facts and/or objective explanation we or anyone else can offer. Throughout our existence, and at its deepest and richest levels, we always know more than we can articulate.

All of this is true at the theoretic and/or scientific levels of knowledge as well. Deep thinkers in any field must continually make judgments and draw conclusions that they cannot fully articulate or justify at the time. Moreover, even when they can provide explicit expression and rationale for their theoretic choices and distinctions, they do so on the basis of skills and other cognitive abilities they have acquired through practice but which they can neither formulate nor justify. Certain assumptions and commitments have to be made, as well, about the possibility and desirability of knowledge, before any explicit knowledge can be obtained, and these assumptions and commitments themselves can only be affirmed and accredited, not justified. All of which leads to the conclusion that the tacit range of the cognitivity continuum is not only a viable one, but that it is logically prior to or more fundamental than the explicit range. For, while some knowing remains essentially and exclusively tacit in character, *all* explicit knowing is rooted in tacit knowing and cannot exist apart from it. The arrow pointing toward explicit knowing in the previous diagram is meant to indicate this primordial priority of tacit knowing.

From an epistemological point of view the crucial question is, to be sure: How is tacit knowing to be confirmed as knowledge if it cannot be formulated and/or justified explicitly? Clearly, not *all* claims to tacit knowing are vindicated, and we cannot allow *every* belief to be affirmed. It must be remembered, however, that not all claims to *explicit* knowledge are acceptable, either. The central concern here is the question of criteria. To begin with, as has been mentioned before, the processes and criteria of evaluation in cases of explicit knowing are themselves only possible within the structure provided by common theories, definitions, and purposes. Facts, conclusions, and the methods of ascertaining them are not just lying around waiting to be stumbled over. Rather, they emerge out of the shared activity and commitments of those who participate in the particular discipline involved. These activities and commitments are never themselves fully defined nor justified; they develop and are vindicated in and through their own existence, rooted as they are in our common tacit knowings.

Tacit knowledge is not self-authenticating, but rather it proves itself valuable and viable in the warp and weft of everyday and theoretic activity, as it is *embodied* in the decisions and doings of our shared tasks, intentions, and institutions. The explicit criteria for evaluating scientific and philosophical knowledge claims (evidence, inference, precision, etc.) are neither self-authenticating nor justifiable in terms of themselves without engaging in circular reasoning. They are justified because of and by their grounding in our *commitments* to reasonableness, consistency, and clarity. The value and veracity of these commitments *show* themselves, and are demonstrated, in the long-term and broad results thereof, even though they may not be *sayable* explicitly. The same holds true for individual claims to tacit knowing as well. Their truth will reveal itself in the quality and consistency of our lives; their lack of truth in the opposite results.

There are three further aspects of our discussion of tacit knowing which bear special mention. First, it is important to acknowledge the somatic or *bodily* basis of tacit knowledge, along with its ramifications for the issue of evaluation. The entire history of Western thought has systematically ignored or scorned the role of the body in human living and knowing, focusing almost exclusively on explicit conceptual formulations and criteria. Even empiricists, for all their emphasis on sensory experience, usually end up stressing "ideas" or "sense data" as the "objects of understanding." The fact remains that we attend *from* our bodies, both kinesthetically and perceptually, *to* the various concepts and reasonings which comprise explicit knowing. All of the skills involved in explicit knowledge, whether those involved in observation or those necessary to theoretic reasoning, are initially learned through bodily imitation and practice, through muscular, auditory, and oral activity. Thus the tacit—and the somatic—base of all knowing. We do not, and cannot, articulate exhaustively how these factors function in the knowing process before we become involved in them—even such an articulation would have to make *use* of them. All knowledge pivots around and flows from the embodied character of our existence.[12]

Two further aspects of tacit knowing need to be discussed before moving on to a consideration of the implications of this epistemological revolution for religious belief in general and Christian faith in particular. The crux of the traditional, critical definition of knowledge is the notion of inference, either deductive (as with logic) or inductive (as with science). The process of moving from premises or observational data to conclusions in a way that can be replicated and checked by others is the hallmark of modern epistemological endeavor. There can be no denying the value of this procedure, but I would insist that as a complete (not to say dogmatic) account of the nature of knowledge it falls significantly short. For here again we confront the problem that not every aspect or basis of such explicit factors can be articulated apart from a tacit structure and grounding. The inferential process is only viable and applicable within predefined parameters and commitments—to rules of consistency and clarity—which can themselves only be justified in terms of the dynamic of tacit knowing. Thus, not all knowledge claims can be explicated in terms of the inferential process.

Tacit knowing on the other hand is characterized by what Michael Polanyi called *"integrative acts."* In a manner helpfully described and documented by Gestalt psychologists of perception, the knower discerns and grasps wholes or "comprehensive realities" in their completeness *prior* to being able to analyze the particular parts thereof. This act of cognitive closure is what enables us to find and bestow meaning in our perceptual and conceptual activity. If we did not first grasp wholes, at some general though vague level, we would never be able to recognize the parts thereof as *parts* of anything, and would thus be left to a continual bombardment of discrete but meaningless particulars. This crucial integrative activity, which is more fundamental than the inductive process, is not reversible. Once one has grasped a whole, be it a face or a linguistic meaning, it is impossible to retrace one's steps as if the whole had not yet been grasped. Moreover, this integrative act arises out of the interaction between our subsidiary awareness and bodily activity, so it is essentially tacit in character.

Third, it is imperative that we realize how the traditional, especially modern, approach to knowledge "objectifies" that which is known. Of course, as has been noted, there are contexts and tasks to which separation between the knower and the known is appropriate, but only as an abstract and temporary technique to facilitate analysis. Both the Heisenberg principle of indeterminacy and Gestalt psychology have established that our interaction with that which we know cannot be ignored in any account of the basis of and test for knowledge. Reality is not experienced as a collection of inert, individual particulars that can be observed and analyzed from a distance with detachment. Our acknowledgement of the tacit character and logically prior nature of the dynamic between subsidiary awareness and bodily activity fits with this account of experience and knowledge, thereby overcoming the dichotomy between the knower and the known. In tacit knowing the knower and the known are the symbiotic poles of a *relational* context. This relationality involves an interaction between the two, a two-way give-and-take between reality and the searching mind. It is important, of course, to distinguish between relationality and identity, between the interaction between and the union of the knower and the known. Mysticism is not being advocated.

An understanding of the tacit grounding of all knowing, especially in regard to the richer and more mediated dimensions of experience, is very valuable, indeed, when thinking about the nature of Christian belief. My basic proposal is that we come to think of religious knowing as essentially *tacit* in character. It arises out of the deep and unarticulatable interaction between our subsidiary awareness of God's mediated revelatory activity (in nature, history, and community) and our own existential and ethical (behavioral) search for reality, meaning, and truth. When this interaction yields comprehensive and meaningful wholes, both commitment and a desire for explicit articulation result. Thus both the Christian way of life and a development of a Christian theology grow out of our religious experience, both personal and social, and out of our response to it as embodied and conceptual beings. Religious knowing is now seen as primarily experiential, at the tacit level, a matter of discernment and commitment coming first and theological articulation coming second.

In addition, I would suggest, the bridge or vehicle between the tacit and the explicit in religious knowing is the *metaphoric mode*. The deep and abiding metaphors that lie at the center of Christian experience and community (such as redemption, incarnation, kingdom, servanthood, and resurrection) embody and mediate our tacit awareness and understanding of spiritual reality, while serving as the matrix out of which our more explicit, conceptual understandings are formulated.

Since these explicit articulations are always dependent on but can never fully express the tacit discernments, it follows that theology, while both inevitable and valuable, is both secondary and approximate in relation to faith and practice. Moreover, the conception of religious knowing as *tacit* is highly appropriate to our previous understanding of reality as a hierarchy of *mediated* dimensions, and spiritual meaning as essentially *metaphoric* in character. These three notions together form a model of Christian faith and understanding that is, in my view, both highly coherent and fruitful, while at the same time being solidly biblical and incarnational.

Most of the history of Western theology has resulted from the prereflective adoption of the philosophical bias toward explicit, conceptual knowing as the only legitimate form of knowledge. The upshot has been a dominant tendency to define belief in terms of mental assent to certain doctrinal formulations or as a purely personal "leap of faith," as with the existentialist overreaction to such undue intellectualization. I am not trying to minimize the importance of explicit conceptualization in religious contexts, but only to place it in perspective in relation to the deeper and prior mode of religious knowing, namely the tacit dimension of religious awareness and commitment.

One of the important ramifications of this shift from viewing Christian faith as exclusively, or even primarily, a conceptual matter to that of a more holistic, experiential and tacit dynamic is the possibility of overcoming the long and well-established bias in Christendom against the human body. The dualism between soul and body, adopted by Christian thinkers unduly influenced by platonic doctrines, is completely out of harmony with both the Incarnation ("the Word became flesh") and the notion of the resurrection of the body at the completion of the redemptive process. It is time Christians took the embodied nature of their own existence and the gospel message seriously, and the primordial character of tacit knowing is of significant help in so doing.

Along with this "postcritical" understanding of the nature

of religious knowing as essentially tacit rather than explicit in character, goes a shift from thinking of it as based in the inferential process toward conceiving of it as grounded in *integrative acts.* Since religious knowing is not primarily a matter of giving mental assent to certain explicit propositions, its basis need not and cannot be seen as a compiling of indisputable evidence or premises from which necessary or even highly probable conclusions can be said to follow. Rather, religious knowing arises out of our interaction with God's mediated revelatory activity at the tacit and deepest levels of our existence, where reality and the sincere search for it encounter each other. This interaction gives rise to integrative acts wherein our discernments of truth form meaningful wholes and from which flow both appropriate behavior and the theological enterprise. This explains why in the face of intellectual challenges and difficulties at the explicit level, significant though they be, religious believers tend to remain confident of the ultimate truth of their insights and commitments. This distinction should not be abused, however, thereby giving license to naïveté and cognitive dishonesty. Faith must be responsible.

Here the essentially *relational* character of religious knowing in general and Christian faith in particular becomes extremely significant. God, the "object" of religious knowing, is not to be known by means of objective detachment, but can only be encountered through open and sincere interaction at the deep, tacit levels of our existence. At this level, the primordial ground of all knowledge, the knower and the known are not two distinct entities separated by an epistemological gap bridged only by inference and probability. Rather, they are symbiotically interrelated by mutual participation one with another. Revelation is God's redemptive activity in the life of humanity, while faith is our discernment of and response to that activity. This response, to be sure, leads to concrete behavior patterns and explicit conceptual systems, but these are not the basis of religious knowing; they are its fruit, and as such they must be under constant modification as the individual and cultural contexts change.

A final word. Since, at the deepest level, claims to religious knowing are tacit in character, testing them becomes a question of evaluating such things as: (1) the *correspondence* between the primordial insight at the center of the commitment and the ensuing behavioral patterns of the individual or community involved; (2) the *coherence* of the relation between the pivotal metaphors of the faith under consideration and the explicit theological formulations which flow from them; and (3) the *fruitfulness* of the above factors in producing increased richness and growth, in both stability and creativity, in the lives of the participants. These may seem like extremely vague and relative criteria for gauging the value and truth of religious belief to those who have been raised and/or trained to think according to the standard, critical mode of understanding so dominant in Western thought. I can only reply that though they are far from "objective" and "precise," such criteria are the only ones deep, broad, and flexible enough to do justice to the most profound levels and issues of existence with which we humans must deal. On the one hand, such criteria are essentially those we employ when making the big decisions of life with responsibility, whether in choosing a mate or a political posture. On the other hand, they are far more concrete and measurable, more public and experiential, than anything offered by those who would suggest that Christian faith is totally personal and/or subjective.

Suggested Reading

Berger, Peter. *A Rumor of Angels.* Garden City, NY: Doubleday, 1970.

Carnell, E. J. *Christian Commitment.* New York: Macmillan, 1957.

Hick, John. *Faith and Knowledge.* New York: Cornell Univ. Press, 1966.

Polanyi, Michael. *The Tacit Dimension.* Garden City, NY: Doubleday, 1966.

Purtill, Richard. *Thinking About Religion.* Englewood Cliffs, NJ: Prentice-Hall, 1978.

Trueblood, Elton. *Philosophy of Religion.* New York: Harper & Row, 1957.

A Retrospective: 8
Confidence and Humility

I AM AFRAID I MUST APOLOGIZE for the long-windedness of the preceding chapter. It is difficult to know how to say enough without saying too much. Also, in trying not to be too long one is forced to be condensed and abstract. I hope, however, that the reader has arrived at this point with more than a modicum of appreciation for the depth of the problems involved and for the potential of a "postcritical" posture for dealing with them. The purpose of this final chapter is to offer a brief review of the major issues faced in the earlier chapters from the perspective provided by the fresh approach sketched in the preceding chapter. I shall conclude with a reminder about the importance of continuing this dialogue between "Athens and Jerusalem" in the proper spirit.

Each of the challenges raised by the various academic disciplines in relation to Christian faith is slightly different from the others, depending on the particular issues and angles of approach involved. Therefore some aspects of the perspective provided by the fresh proposal will be more relevant than others to the various disciplines and challenges taken up in our previous discussion. Nevertheless, there is a deep sense in which all of the difficulties introduced flow from a common source, namely from a fairly well-integrated set of assumptions that form the Modern or critical point of view. In addition, therefore, the overall posture being proposed in these pages speaks, as a whole, to each of these difficulties to some relevant degree.

In the chapter on the natural sciences, the fundamental issue under discussion was that of *reductionism*. There is a tendency for the scientific mind-set to seek to explain every phenomenon or level of existence, in terms of successively simpler ones, until the whole of reality has been accounted for in terms of one basic, irreducible mode or level. This tendency is understandable, even admirable, since there is something inherently reasonable about seeking the simplest, most comprehensive explanation of things. However, it is unreasonable to carry this effort to such an extreme that one must force reality to fit a preconceived schema. It would seem that natural scientists have frequently been guilty of such forcing, especially when it comes to explaining the origin and development of life.

However, the best way to combat reductionism is not to insist that spiritual reality and the human level of life are by nature inherently above and entirely distinct from other, more natural levels. Such dualistic supernaturalism has not fared very well in producing a convincing case against various forms of reductionism, primarily because it is based not on a Judeo-Christian understanding of God's relation to the world, but on one borrowed from classical Greek philosophy. A far better, more flexible, and fruitful understanding flows from the adoption of the notion of *mediated dimensions* as the fundamental structure of reality. This model negates reductionism without resorting to the static dualism of traditional supernaturalism.

It will be recalled that the first aspect of the fresh, post-critical posture proposed in the preceding chapter was an understanding of reality as comprised of simultaneously interpenetrating dimensions arranged according to a mediational hierarchy of richness and comprehensiveness. This hierarchical structure enables us to account for the concept of *emergence*—one level or dimension of reality arising out of but emcompassing more than those "beneath" it—without either reductionistic or dualistic implications. Each successively richer dimension must conform to the *boundary conditions* set by the previous, less rich dimensions—as with physics in relation to chemistry, for instance—while transcending those dimensions in complexity and comprehensiveness. Organic life and human existence, for example, both transcend without contradicting inorganic and other biological principles, respectively.

Such a dimensional model of reality enables us to think and talk about God's creative and redemptive activity in relation to the world in a manner that allows for transcendence (contra reductionism) without giving rise to the difficulties of proving supernatural "intrusions" (contra dualism). Creation and redemption come *in and through* natural and historical processes; they are neither reducible to them nor entirely above them. As it is possible to discern an author's or artist's intentions in and through the particulars of his or her work—though there remains, to be sure, room for differing interpretations here—so it is possible to speak of discerning God's activity in relation to the world in and through its particulars and patterns. There are, of course, no unarguable proofs here, as there are none with respect to any of the more significant dimensions and decisions of human life. One cannot "prove" that God is active, any more than one can "prove" that democracy is better than totalitarianism, but this does not mean that it is impossible to distinguish responsible interpretations and decisions from irresponsible ones in such situations.

This *mediational* understanding of God's action in relation to the world not only keeps alive the possibility of meaningful discussion of teleological patterns in human history and society. It also provides a way of thinking about the notion of miracles which also avoids the hard-and-fast dichotomy between naturalism and supernaturalism. God's action in the world need not be seen as an intrusion of divine power into the laws of nature and the like in order to be taken seriously. Not only is there more interrelation between natural patterns

of behavior and God's involvement in the world than traditional supernaturalism entails—after all, it is God's world in
the first place—but miracles can be seen as unusual, seemingly unexplainable events in which can be discerned a special pattern of significance for the believing community. In a
word, God's activity can be helpfully understood as *mediated*
in and through the natural world.

This same mediational pattern may be applied with profit
to the notion of *revelation* and to the phenomenon of the Judeo-Christian Scriptures. The model here is the Incarnation.
God's pattern of self-revelation prior to and in Christ is *in and
through* the events of history and community, not over and
above them. "The Word became flesh and dwelt among us,"
not as a supernatural being from another world *disguised* as a
human (like Superman disguised as the mild-mannered re-
porter for the Daily Planet), but as a real, concrete human
being, and yet as "more." This "more" was mediated in and
through Christ's person—his being and doing—not superim-
posed on it from above. In like fashion, the Scriptures, as the
record, response, and interpretation of God's revelatory activity, were themselves mediated in and through the cultures,
languages, peoples, and events of their time, albeit in such a
way as to continue to speak authentically for those of subsequent times and alternative places.

Moving on to our discussion of the social sciences, the
central issue there was *relativism*. It is true, of course, that
here again we encounter reductionism in its behavioristic,
functionalistic, and Marxist variations. Although the permutations and progressions are slightly different in these areas
of concern, I am of the opinion that once again the notion of
reality arranged according to mediational dimensions of increasing richness and comprehensiveness goes a long way
toward meeting the difficulties by these versions of reductionism. I touched on these possibilities in chapter 3 and the
basic line of approach should be clear from the above considerations, so I shall not treat the matter further here. There are

other issues more integral to the social sciences to be dealt with at this juncture.

The *"objectivism"* of much of the work done in the social sciences does need to be faced. In both chapters 3 and 7, I tried to indicate what seem to be the inherent difficulties of carrying the standard of objectivity too far. We cannot, after all, be entirely "objective" about our commitment to objectivity; but this does not mean that we are inconsistent or that all our efforts to obtain real knowledge are doomed from the start. All that is necessary for a consistent and fruitful understanding of knowledge, together with its basis and criteria, is accrediting our own fundamental commitments and capacities as the axis around which our scientific efforts revolve. Such an axis needs no external, objective justification other than its own necessity and usefulness. We simply must acknowledge the personal and social basis of our epistemological quest, structured as it is by the tasks of human existence and by our commitment to the truth. In exposing the "cult of objectivism" we also exorcise the "ghost of subjectivism."

The *relativism* inherent within the study of human behavior, whether on the individual, cultural, or historical level, is not unrelated to the epistemological issues raised in the above paragraph. As I indicated in chapter 3, I believe the humility and tolerance reflected in the concern of the social scientist to avoid ethnocentrism and arrogance is to be commended. Far too long those of us in the West—scientists, philosophers, and theologians alike—have carried on our work as if other cultures and modes of thought and life were immature and/or perverse. There are, however, serious limitations to such tolerance when carried to an extreme, and it is important to speak to them from the perspective provided by the epistemological dimension of the postcritical posture introduced in the previous chapter.

It is simply impossible to go all the way with any form of relativism without undercutting one's own position. For the assertion that all views and practices are relative is itself a *view* and a form of behavior, and if all such things are relative, then so is relativism—which renders it devoid of absolute or universal truth value. It is clear, however, that anyone asserting relativism, or any other scientific view about human life, desires that assertion to be true, not relative to this culture and time period, but absolutely. Science, after all, aims at general descriptions of "how things are," *period*. In short, the search for knowledge in any field presupposes a common commitment to truth in some universal sense, what Polanyi called "universal intent." Such a commitment rules out any form of extreme relativism.

Thus it is that the social sciences must acknowledge *both* that knowledge is not, and need not be, completely objective *and* that it is not, and cannot be, completely relative. Further, it must acknowledge that the human study of human beings, even more than the study of nature, is both highly complex and *relational*. Here, clearly, the known and the knower are engaged in interaction, since the latter can only come to an understanding of the former form within it. This "only" must be taken in two senses: first, in this case the knower is *part* of what is being studied; and second, it is *only* by being human that knowledge of humanity can be acheived. The capacities and skills, the concepts and commitments we bring to the study of human life and society are, after all, the very things we are studying—unless, of course, we pretend that human behavior is no different from other animal behavior. But such pretending completely undercuts the very notion of human *knowledge* as such, and thus it undercuts science as well.

The Christian understanding of knowledge, whether of humanity or divinity or the relation between them, is in harmony with all of the affirmations noted above. Clearly, it sees true knowledge as relational. In addition, a Christian epistemology will readily acknowledge the universal intent that drives and guides our efforts to know and understand God and our interaction therewith. Moreover, in my view, the Christian will also affirm that no matter how careful, sincere, and bright we are, our knowledge of God is always partial and subject to distortion. This is not only because we are limited, but because divine revelation is mediated in and through personal, historical, and cultural factors. Christian knowledge of God is incarnational, after all, and thus it is "through a glass, darkly." Revelation is *qualitatively* absolute, and thus sufficient for our needs, but it is not *quantitatively* absolute, that is, exhaustive or completed.

Another way of putting this last point, one that flows directly from the posture presented in chapter 7, is to say that although our knowledge of God is adequate and firm at the tacit level, it must always be approximate and flexible at the explicit level. Thus in our personal and communal life we may have confidence that our commitments are viable and true, while in the theological and moral sphere we must remain humble and open to new truth. Some of this new truth may, in fact, come by means of our study of human life and society—if we pay heed to the parameters we have suggested in the foregoing discussion.

Turning now to our previous consideration of the humanities, the central difficulty there was *humanism.* The modern tendency to seek to explain the world and human existence strictly in terms of a horizontal model, without any reference to a vertical, transcendent reality, does indeed stand in conflict with an important aspect of Christian faith. However, as I indicated in chapter 4, I do not think the traditional dualistic or realmistic approach is the most helpful way to meet this challenge. For this move just raises all the standard difficulties concerning the criteria and rationale for establishing the reality of such a "higher" realm, as well as for confirming its "intrusions" into our human realm. Such difficulties simply lead to all-too-familiar and irresolvable statements.

It is precisely at this juncture that the notion of *mediated dimensions* is so useful, for it gives us a way to speak and think about spiritual reality and its interaction with our existence that preserves the possibility of transcendence without rendering it so mysterious and problematic. To continue with the spatial way of speaking, the dimensional model provides a kind of "depth" that neither horizontalism nor verticalism can offer. In addition, it accounts for the interaction between and among the dimensions, by means of the concept of mediation, which is left unaccounted for by vertical dualism. A mediated discernment is neither read *off* the flat surface of experience nor read *into* from above. Rather, it is read *out of* the patterns and mysteries of experience, yielding an awareness and knowledge of that which is being mediated which can neither be reduced to nor separated from the particulars of that experience.

This notion of mediated dimensions leads to an understanding of reality and experience that is at once naturalistic and humanistic on the one hand and "more" than that on the other hand. It is in harmony with the Judeo-Christian view of God's creation of the world and of the divine image in humanity. Theologians used to speak of the knowledge of God which results from such mediation as, "natural" or "general revelation," and I am quite comfortable with this notion. Even special or historical revelation is, after all, mediated in character, as the Incarnation clearly indicates. There is such a thing, then, as "Christian humanism," if by this term one signifies the revelatory and redemptive activity of God *in and through* the life of humanity. The affirmation of such activity in human existence, of course, neither requires nor allows for an equation of two; it simply maintains their relatedness and invites our discernment of the one in and through the other.

The quest for meaning which so characterizes the humanities, whether in its linguistic or existential form (as with analytic and existentialist philosophies, respectively), can be and has been spoken to (in chapter 4) in terms of wider views of language and existence. The later Wittgenstein has led the way with respect to the former, while Christian existentialists have set the pace with respect to the latter. Moreover, in chapter 7 I tried to indicate more specifically how an emphasis on the metaphoric mode of expression, together with an acknowledgement of the primordial and tacit nature of commitment and knowledge, brings about a deeper and more fruitful understanding of the quest for meaning and truth.

At bottom I see the concern with linguistic meaning, especially at the level focused by Wittgenstein, and the stress on
meaning in existence, as taken up by phenomenology, to be
essentially on to the same thing. They are both seeking an
understanding of the character and structure of human existence at its deepest level. It is here that I find Polanyi's
thought so fascinating and worthwhile, for in his work with
tacit knowing lie the distinctions and insights necessary for
synthesizing the emphasis of the analytic and existentialist
philosophies. Tacit knowing explains the primordial nature
of both linguistic meaning and human commitment, while at
the same time providing a schema that integrates these two
concerns. Both language and existence can only be understood as the fruit of our common, relational interaction
around shared needs and goals.

The Christian, both as a person and as a thinker, cannot
help but have deep interest in both aspects of the quest for
meaning that characterizes our age. After all, the central
thrust of religious belief is toward authentic existence, which
is realized, in the Christian view, through sincere and faithful
relationship with God as Creator and Redeemer. The New
Testament term for salvation has at its root the notion of
health and making whole. Christian faith is, in this sense,
humanistic because its goal is the fulfillment of the original
creative intentions of God for humankind. Thus any philosophy which seeks authentic existence, such as existentialism, is
an ally, at least in this respect. There are, as we have noted,
further discriminations to be made between various kinds of
and difficulties with existentialism.

Likewise, it is no accident that the most common metaphor
for revelation in the Judeo-Christian Scriptures is that of language. Genesis begins with God creating the world by speaking, and throughout the Old Testament, God's interaction
with humankind in general and the nation Israel in particular
is cast in the dialogical mode: "Hear, oh Israel . . . ," "The
Word of the Lord came . . . ," "Here am I, O Lord . . . ," and
so on. In the New Testament, God's part in this dialogue is

expressed in the divine *Word's* becoming flesh, the ultimate embodiment of God's redemptive activity in relation to humankind. The Scriptures themselves are also, of course, embodied words—communications through written *languages* of the reality and meaning of God's love and purposes for people.

Moreover, because the Scriptures are written in human languages (and they would be of no use to us if they were not), they can only speak of God in terms which both build on but point beyond human experience. In short, the Scriptures' primary mode of discourse is the metaphoric mode. The characterizations of God as King, Shepherd, Mother Eagle, Judge, and Lover throughout the Old Testament, and Jesus' parables and Paul's rich images of redemption, the bride and body of Christ, and so forth in the New Testament, make this amply clear. Therefore, those of us who wish properly to interpret the Scriptures, in order to participate more fully in the love and life embodied therein, have a great stake in coming to an in-depth understanding of the nature and implications of metaphoric language. That this mode of expression operates primarily in the tacit dimension of existence and knowledge should be of equal importance and interest to the Christian who seeks a richer faith.

It is time now to reconsider briefly the issues which arose from our discussion of the relation between Christian faith and the arts. The chief difficulty here was with *subjectivism*, and in at least two senses of the term. In one sense, subjectivism means that there are no objective criteria by means of which to judge the meaning and value of art: "beauty is in the eye of the beholder." In a different sense, this term is used to characterize the tendency of modern artists to create works which give expression to their own inner feelings, rather than represent the objective world. My overall approach to this question is to urge a more tolerant and reflective consideration of the processes and particulars involved in artistic creation. Specifically, I would submit that the values embodied in works of art are more "objective" than the "subjectivist" cry would lead us to think.

In chapter 7 I presented the notion of mediating and mediated dimensions as a fresh and fruitful way of thinking about experienced reality. This model can be applied with profit to our understanding of aesthetic awareness and value. In a work of art, whether visual, tactile, or literary, the meanings, moods, and "message" are mediated to the "prehender" (you and me) by means of the particular features which comprise the work. The lines, shapes, colors, tones, rhythms, textures, images, and so on, bear within them, and within their concrete configurations, richer and broader signification. The various values, such as sadness, tension, and harmony, are not found in one corner, measure, or chapter, but they are mediated in and through the particulars. They are "more" than the particulars but dependent on them, for both their existence and our awareness of them.

In my own teaching of film appreciation I suggest a three-fold schema for enhancing our awareness and understanding of film as an art form. First, there is the *perceptual* level: the images, colors, shades, movements (including those of the camera), editing techniques (fades, cuts, etc.), sounds, film texture, and the like. We begin by noting and talking about these, since this is the level most people generally ignore. Next, there is the *dramatic* level: the setting, characters, structure, plot, dialogue, and such. Here we use standard literary and dramatic interpretive techniques, although one must be careful not to force these on what is primarily a visual art form. Thirdly, we take up the *metaphoric* level: What does film "mean," for the characters within it, for us as individual viewers, and for human existence in general? It is very important to refrain from dealing with this level until the others have been explored in some depth, because each richer, more comprehensive level is mediated through the one(s) beneath it.

The general pattern of this approach goes a long way toward overcoming the charge of subjectivism in the arts because it establishes modes and criteria for interpretation. While not yielding "objective" conclusions (which, as we have seen, are a will-o'-the-wisp anyway, even in natural science, apart from a stipulated context), such interpretive techniques and principles do establish a general ground and range for common meaning and value. Even though there are many viable interpretive angles for a given work of art, and this is a mark of its significance, there is not an unlimited number and some can be shown to be better than others, within specific contexts or time periods.

In my view, the religious value of the above understanding of art is considerable. For frequently people claim that religion is every bit as subjective as art. It is my counter-claim that when the notions of religious awareness in general and revelation in particular are viewed from within the foregoing discussion of aesthetic value, they can be seen to have a solidity and viability in human experience which renders tham anything but subjective. To be sure, there is room for a wide variety of interpretations of and within religious belief, but some are more helpful and meaningful than others—and the ongoing dialogue about which and why is itself of tremendous value.

More specifically, I would suggest that the Christian concept of incarnation follows precisely those mediational patterns inherent within aesthetic expression and awareness. God, as the divine artist, embodies the divine character and purpose for human life in the person and activity of Jesus of Nazareth. This revelation is neither explicit nor essentially conceptual; rather, it is *mediated* to us in and through the particulars that comprise the character, life, and teachings of Jesus. Its meaning does not simply lie on the surface, but can only be encountered and appropriated by means of sincere interaction and participation—in other words, by means of faith and faithfulness. At the same time, revelation is not "heavyhanded"; its mediational quality creates an existential "space" that both respects our freedom and encourages our responsibility.

Moreover, as with art, so with revelation; we must be careful to start with the concrete particulars in our effort to grasp meaning and value. Far too often we begin at the wrong end, form our abstract conclusions about *how* it must be understood and *what* it must mean, and end up with a dogmatic and irrelevant, if not downright pernicious, interpretive system. Christian theology, in my opinion, must be grounded in the particulars of experience (both individual and corporate) and those of the Scripture. In addition, and contrary to the advice of some, the abstract and systematic aspects of experience and Scripture, while immensely valuable, must always remain secondary in relation to the concrete and narrative aspects as ground and guide for interpretation. To be specific, the particulars of Jesus' person and teaching are the axis around which all other Scripture and theology must orbit.

The main thrust of the foregoing discussion jibes with the other themes taken up in chapter 7, as well as with the mediational theme. A functional, metaphoric understanding of symbolic communication, whether in artistic or religious expression, befits a dimensionally structured reality wherein the richer dimensions are mediated through the less rich. In both art and religion a proper dynamic balance (as distinguished from a static balance) must be struck between the conventional use of symbols and fresh, creative uses of them. To lean too heavily on convention is to confine and eventually kill. To become overly unconventional is to fail to communicate. Those who would seek to communicate God's richness through symbols will do well to reflect on the fact that we have no record of Jesus ever using the same metaphor or image (such as "born again") more than once.

In a similar way, the notion of tacit knowing also befits a mediational understanding of reality and metaphoric communication. Our discernment of aesthetic meaning and value is mediated in and through our subsidiary awareness of and our bodily interaction with the particulars of a given work of art. Our senses funnel and integrate the sights, sounds, motion, and touches we take in, giving rise to tacit knowledge of the patterns and meanings thereof. Out of this tacit integration arise our attempts to express and communicate insights and outlooks in symbolic form. Metaphors, both sensory and linguistic, are created, which in turn give rise to more explicit, conceptual modes of communication. Religious awareness and symbolic expression follow essentially the same dynamic, moving from the tacit toward the explicit by means of mediational and integrative processes at the deepest levels of our being, both individually and in community.

Finally, we return to our consideration of world religions in relation to Christian faith. The central issue here is *pluralism*. The reality and vitality of religions other than Christianity is a relatively new phenomenon for Christians, one which calls for a more creative and, I believe, more truly Christian posture than either traditional exclusivism or modern inclusivism. It simply will no longer do (if it ever did) to exclude everyone who has never heard of Jesus of Nazareth from the love and redemptive activity of God. Nor will it do to blandly *include* everyone who practices a religion, with no regard to the concrete differences in their varying qualities of faith and practice. In addition to the considerations I offered in chapter 6, especially those dealing with Jesus' attitude toward the faith of "outsiders," certain of the themes presented in the previous chapter seem to me to be helpful in the following ways.

The general understanding of the functional and metaphoric character of language opens up both the necessity and the possibility of construing religious language much more broadly than has traditionally been done. Until fairly recently almost all of the thinking about and dialogue between Christianity and other religions has been conducted on the assumption that the chief differences were focused in doctrinal *propositions*, and that the central task was to see which of these, if any, might be harmonized, reinterpreted, set aside as secondary, etc. Exclusivists insisted on certain Christian doctrines' being unique, while inclusivists looked for a common core of teachings among the many. Even today many of those working in this field continue to assume that the linguistic expressions and beliefs of the different religions are essentially propositional in nature.

Not only do the insights of cultural anthropologists and historians of religion belie any such one-dimensional view of religious belief, as was pointed out in chapter 6, but those of linguistic philosophy and the phenomenology of language do so as well. Language is now viewed as a multidimensional mode of expression arising from within the highly complex social activity of human beings as they seek to interact with and understand the world in which they find themselves. Propositions, as representations of factual situations, certainly have their place within this rich mix of activity, but only as they function toward the accomplishment of the broader, more fundamental tasks and purposes of life. Propositional speech-acts grow out of ordinary language, which is wonderfully and bewilderingly diverse and "open-textured," not the other way around.

All of this applies with immeasurable force to the understanding of religious discourse in general and to the question of pluralism in particular. Even though propositional speech figures into most, if not all, religions in important ways, it is imperative to remember that it does not function as an end in itself. Rather, they work within the concrete contexts and activities of the believing community as it worships and serves God. This not only means that the propositional utterances of a given religion can only properly be understood in relation to these contexts and activities, but that the other dimensions of religious language present therein may well be more fundamental. People speak to and about God, after all, with and to other persons in order to praise, thank, repent, vow, affirm, share, baptize, marry, confess, etc. —not in order to list abstract truths.

One of the chief uses of God-talk, whether one is speaking with believers or nonbelievers, is to *evoke* a discernment of and commitment to divine reality and activity. Thus, even credal and doctrinal propositions are frequently employed as a means of enhancing the quality of our own and others' awareness of and participation in God's love. Various metaphors and parables, analogies and theoretical models are used to these ends, and their propositional dimension is only one among the many aspects of religious linguistic activity. It is precisely this aspect of the religious pluralism issue that must be addressed and explored if the dialogue between Christian and non-Christian believers is to proceed in a meaningful and profitable fashion. Further, it is most likely here that the greatest commonality among faiths is to be found, since they all share to some degree in the human need and capacity for an authentic relationship with the source and goal of existence. We are all created, after all, in the image of God.

Shifting to epistemological concerns, the concept of tacit knowing makes it possible for us to speak of a common integration of subsidiary awareness of divine reality at the experiential level within all religions. Even though this tacit integration may well yield different metaphoric and doctrinal expressions at the explicit level, from one religion to the next, it is possible and even likely that that of which differing religions are aware is in some sense the same. We do live a common form of life as human beings, after all, and we do live in an essentially similar world. Also, Christians, as well as adherents to many other major religions, believe that everything flows from a common source. At any rate, such possibilities render inter-faith dialogue viable, and this dialogue is essential to the responsible treatment of the reality and importance of pluralism.

There is, to be sure, no guarantee that the use of the post-critical understanding of language and knowledge will eliminate all the differences between and among the world's major religions. It may not even be desirable to do away with such differences, at least at the historical and cultural level, for distinctive forms of religious expressions are both inevitable and valuable in their own right. Nevertheless, greater understanding of and respect for one another's faith is indeed a necessity in our pluralistic context, and the postcritical posture at least facilitates such a dialogical approach. Moreover, at the *most* the postcritical model may provide a way of integrating Christian faith with other religions which avoids both exclusivism and inclusivism, while enhancing and enriching our overall understanding of and appreciation for religious belief as such.

All of which brings us to the end of our postcritical review of the main fields of study and the major issues arising between them and Christian faith. In addition, we are also at the conclusion of our entire dialogical apologetic. I hope it has been an interesting and worthwhile exploration of the problems and possibilities involved in the encounter between Athens and Jerusalem. And I also hope it has and will continue to be a springboard for the reader's further consideration of and interaction with these issues, together with their ramifications for Christian faith. Before concluding, let me underscore once again the two attitudes which, in my view, not only *can* be conjoined but *must* be conjoined in a proper and fruitful understanding of Christian faith in relation to the search for truth.

First, *confidence*. Faith is nothing if it does not involve confidence. In addition, to believe something is necessarily to believe that it is true. Clearly, people would not be Christians if they had not found an experiential and reflective ground for their faith, whatever the level of maturity involved. But confidence does not entail arrogance or dogmatism. No matter how mature our understanding or how firm our conviction, there is always the possibility—perhaps even the necessity—of our faith's growing. Spiritual growth *always* involves modification—and struggle—otherwise it is not growth, but merely the rearrangement of our prejudices. Real faith always remains open to fresh truth (as Peter's vision on the rooftop clearly indicates), trusting in God's vast wisdom and integrity.

Which brings us to the second crucial characteristic of a vital faith, *humility*. Some people think there is a contradiction between confidence and humility, but such a view confuses the former with credulity and bias, while mistaking the latter for "wishy-washiness." A confessional stance, on the other hand, enables us to confess commitment with enthusiasm and confidence, while at the same time acknowledging that we, too, are only human and have a great deal to learn—both *for* ourselves and *from* others. I would submit that confidence and humility, rather than being opposites, go hand-in-hand for a faith that is both responsible and honoring to God.

Much of what I have been trying to say, as much by example as by speech, boils down to the simple ideas that: (1) it is necessary and valuable for Christian faith to provide a rationale for itself in relation to the general human search for truth—that is, for the individual believer to "give a reason for the hope that is within" (1 Pet. 3:15)—and that (2) it is *not* necessary or possible for a person, whether a Christian or not, to provide *proof* for his or her belief in order for it to be *responsible* belief. Justified belief must be sincere and open on the one hand, reasonable and responsible on the other hand. Honest Christian faith need not be more and can surely be no less.

Notes

Chapter 2

1. See *Lucy,* Donald Johanson and Maitland Edey (New York: Simon & Schuster, 1981).
2. See *The Immense Journey* (New York: Vintage Books, 1946).
3. See Fritjof Capra, *The Tao of Physics* (Boulder, CO: Shambhala Pubns., 1975).
4. I am drawing here on Michael Polanyi's *The Tacit Dimension* (Chicago: Univ. of Chicago Press, 1966), especially chapter 3.
5. The stark presentation of the case against miracles is found in David Hume's thought. See Richard Wollheim, ed., *Hume on Religion* (New York: World Pubns., 1963).
6. Readers may find helpful C. S. Lewis, *Miracles* (New York: Macmillan, 1955).
7. Here E. J. Carnell's *Christian Commitment* (New York: Macmillan, 1957) should prove helpful.
8. See Ian Barbour, *Myths, Models and Paradigms* (New York: Harper & Row, 1974).
9. See here Thomas Kuhn's *The Structure of Scientific Revolutions* (Chicago: Univ. of Chicago Press, 1962).
10. Ian Ramsey's *Models and Mystery* (New York: Oxford Univ. Press, 1964) is especially good on this topic.

Chapter 3

1. See Skinner's book, *Beyond Freedom and Dignity* (New York: Knopf, 1971).
2. Here Peter Winch's *The Idea of a Social Science* (Atlantic Highlands, NJ: Humanities, 1958) and P. Berger and J. Luckman's *The Social Construction of Reality* (Garden City, NY: Doubleday, 1967) are helpful.
3. See N. R. Hanson, *Patterns of Discovery* (Cambridge: Cambridge Univ. Press, 1958).
4. See Nelson Goodman, *Ways of Worldmaking* (Indianapolis: Hackett Pub., 1980).

5. Michael Polanyi's ideas are being employed here. See his *Knowing and Being* (Chicago: Univ. of Chicago Press, 1969).

6. Polanyi is helpful on this point. See *Knowing and Being*.

7. See E. Durkheim, *The Elementary Forms of the Religious Life* (New York: Collier, 1961).

8. With respect to each of these points I have increasingly found the works of Reinhold Niebuhr to be helpful. See especially his *Moral Man and Immoral Society* (New York: Scribner, 1960).

9. Karl Marx and Friedrich Engels, *On Religion,* ed. Reinhold Niebuhr (New York: Schocken, 1964).

10. Here see Eric Fromm, *Marx's Concept of Man* (New York: Ungar, 1961).

11. See such "liberation theologies" as those of Rubem Alves, *A Theology of Human Hope* (New York: Corpus Books, 1969); Dom Helder Camara, *The Church and Colonialism* (Denville, NJ: Dimension Books, 1969); and James Cone, *A Black Theology* of Liberation (Philadelphia: Lippincott, 1970).

CHAPTER 4

1. Here I am drawing on the insights of Michael Novak in his *Belief and Unbelief* (New York: Macmillan, 1965).

2. A. J. Ayer, *Language, Truth, and Logic* (New York: Dover, 1942).

3. An excellent brief introduction to these can be found in Terrence Tilley's *Talking of God* (New York: Paulist, 1975).

4. In my opinion, the best introduction to both aspects of Wittgenstein's work is Justus Hartnack's *Wittgenstein and Modern Philosophy* (New York: New York Univ. Press, 1965).

5. A book by J. McClendon and J. Smith entitled *Understanding Religious Convictions* (Notre Dame, IN: Univ. of Notre Dame Press, 1965) is an excellent embodiment of this approach.

6. See especially his *Religious Language* (New York: Macmillan, 1955).

7. An excellent guide here is Sallie McFague's *Speaking in Parables* (Philadelphia: Fortress, 1975).

8. A good representative introduction is Walter Kaufmann's *Existentialism from Dostoyevski to Sartre* (New York: New American Library, 1975).

9. Ibid.

10. *Walter Lowrie's A Short Life of Kierkegaard* (Princeton, NJ: Princeton Univ. Press, 1965) is a good introduction.

CHAPTER 5

1. I am relying here on the insights of my friend Donald Weismann. See his *The Visual Arts As Human Experience* (Englewood Cliffs, NJ: Prentice-Hall, 1974).

2. See here Dan Via's *The Parables* (Philadelphia: Fortress, 1967).

3. See B. Lang and F. Williams, eds, *Marxism and Art* (New York: McKay, 1972).

4. I have pursued this thought more thoroughly in my unpublished manuscript, *Art and Incarnation.*

5. In the following discussion I am dependent upon Herbert Reid's *The Meaning of Art* (London: Penguin, 1931).

CHAPTER 6

1. See his *The Reasonableness of Christianity* (London: Adam and Charles Black, 1958).
2. See *On Religion* (New York: Harper & Row, 1958).
3. *The Sacred and the Profane* (New York: Harper & Row, 1957).
4. Carl Jung, *Man and His Symbols* (New York: Dell, 1968).
5. *The Meaning and End of Religion* (New York: Macmillan, 1963).
6. I am here very much indebted to the excellent book by J. McClendon and J. Smith, *Understanding Religious Convictions* (Notre Dame, IN: Univ. of Notre Dame Press, 1965).
7. The writings of H. R. Niebuhr exemplify the approach and are highly recommended. His introduction to *The Responsible Self* (New York: Harper & Row, 1963) is especially helpful.

CHAPTER 7

1. Here again the reader is encouraged to consult my *On Knowing God* (Philadelphia: Westminster, 1981) for a more thorough development of this overall approach.
2. Here again see Thomas Kuhn's *The Structure of Scientific Revolutions* (Chicago: Univ. of Chicago Press, 1970).
3. Here the work of G. H. Mead, *On Social Psychology* (Chicago: Univ. of Chicago Press, 1964) and M. Merleau-Ponty, *Phenomenlogy of Perception* (Atlantic Highlands, NJ: Humanities, 1962) are especially helpful.
4. I find John Hick, *Faith and Knowledge* (Ithaca, NY: Cornell Univ. Press, 1966) and John Oman, *The Natural and the Supernatural* (Cambridge: Cambridge Univ. Press, 1931) very helpful here.
5. See his *Philosophical Investigations* (New York: Macmillan, 1953).
6. Owen Barfield has done an excellent job in his *Poetic Diction* (Middletown, CT: Wesleyan Univ. Press, 1973). See here also C. S. Lewis's essay, "Bluspels and Flalansferes" in *Selected Literary Essays* (Cambridge: Cambridge Univ. Press, 1969).
7. See his *Summa Theologica*, 1.13.
8. *Dynamics of Faith* (New York: Harper & Row, 1957).
9. I highly recommend Sallie MacFague's *Metaphorical Theology* (Philadelphia: Fortress, 1982) in this connection.
10. Dan O. Via's *The Parables* (Philadelphia: Fortress, 1967) is excellent on this topic.
11. In what follows I am very much dependent on the work of Michael Polanyi, especially his *Personal Knowledge* (Chicago: Univ. of Chicago Press, 1958) and *Knowing and Being* (Chicago: Univ. of Chicago Press, 1969).
12. Once again, see Merleau-Ponty's *Phenomenology of Perception* for a powerful presentation of the truth involved here.